Indian Iconography and Religious Tolerance

Indian Iconography and Religious Tolerance

Dr. Sudipa Bandyopadhyay
Associate Professor,
Department of Sanskrit,
Vidyasagar College, and
Visiting faculty,
Department of Sanskrit,
University of Calcutta, Kolkata

MOTILAL BANARSIDASS
INTERNATIONAL
DELHI

First Indian Edition : Delhi, 2025

ISBN : 978-81-98985-42-2 (HB)
ISBN : 978-81-98985-43-9 (PB)

Also available at
MOTILAL BANARSIDASS INTERNATIONAL
H.O. : 41 U.A. Bungalow Road, (Back Lane)Jawahar Nagar, Delhi - 110 007
4261 (basement) Lane #3,Ansari Road, Darya Ganj, New Delhi - 110 002
Shop No. 6, Luz Ginza Complex, 241 Luz Corner, Mylapore, Chennai - 600 004
12/1A, 2nd Floor, Bankim Chatterjee Street, Kolkata - 700 073
Stockist : Motilal Books, Ashok Rajpath, Near Kali Mandir, Patna - 800 004

Printed in India
MOTILAL BANARSIDASS INTERNATIONAL

To

Those artists and their great minds with adept hands that brought into light the concept of religious tolerance of our ancient Indian civilization, through their creative works.

Contents

Preface .... (ix)

Introduction .... (xi)

System of Transliteration .... (xiv)

Abbreviations .... (xvi)

Chapter 1 .... **1**
Origin and Development of Indian Iconography

Chapter 2 .... **11**
Image Worship and Iconography

Chapter 3 .... **23**
Iconography and Communal Harmony

Chapter 4 .... **38**
Indian Iconography

Conclusion 87

Illustrations 89

Bibliography 101

Index 108

Preface

It is well-known to all that the prime ideology of ancient Indian civilization is based on the concept - *vasudhaiva kuṭumbakam*, i.e., 'entire world is to be considered as close relative' which was believed and practiced by our esteemed ancestors from the early Vedic period. Just like every sector of ancient Indian culture and civilization Indian art and iconography has a deep-rooted connection with religious tolerance from the very beginning of the civilization and the ever- increasing pantheons of different sectarian cults will express the significant standpoint on such transformations. That is why, I have started a Research Project on this noble concept through a comparative study to discover the glorious aspect of Indian culture and civilization. Now a days, terrorism caused by religious as well as social intolerance gradually terrorized the day to day life of the common people throughout the world which must be prevented by reminiscing the glorious concept of Universal brotherhood of ancient India and being the torch-bearer of the legacy.

I, therefore, feel to bring such concept followed by our eminent predecessors to the modern world with essential materials from my end. There lies the goal of this work to open the gateway towards the society free of religious fanaticism.

In the preparation of the book, I have received valuable ideas from the renowned work of Professor Jitendra Nath

Banerjee, *The Development of Hindu Iconography* and from the book *Elements of Hindu Iconography* of T.A. Gopinath Rao. I must express my sense of gratitude to my respected teacher Late Professor Amar Chattopadhyay and Late Professor Kalyani Dutta as without their blessings this attempt could not form a complete shape. I am thankful heart and solely to my beloved student, scholar and faculty member Smt. Swatantra Roy who has assisted me with all the technical support and also in preparing the index, in the correction of proof etc. I am conveying my blessings to her and praying for her success and peace to the Almighty God. I have to thank my daughter Dr. Madhuprana Goswami who has always inspired me to devote my time to the present study.

Some blemishes, especially typographical might have crept into this work and for this I crave the indulgence of my readers.

Place: Kolkata
23rd December, 2024

Sudipa Bandyopadhyay

Introduction

In the glorious field of ancient Indian civilization, art and iconography has always been produced in response to a demand, that kind of idealism which would glorify the artist who pursues a personal idea of beauty and strives to express himself. According to the glorious tradition of our ancient civilization, the classification of knowledge is neither universal nor permanent. *Vidyā* (*jñāna* or knowledge) is of four numbers – *Trayī* (*Veda*), *Ānvīkṣikī* (logic and metaphysics along with implementation), *Danḍanīti* (science of governance) and *Vārtā* (agriculture, commerce, technology, medicine, architecture, painting, sculpture etc.). It is also said that, the word, *Śāstra*, has at times been used as a synonym for *Vidyā*, which denotes the instrument of teaching, manual all compendium of rules, religious or scientific treatise. The word *Jñāna* means knowledge and *Vijñāna* stands for the act of distinguishing or discerning, understanding, comprehending and recognizing which means worldly or profane knowledge as distinguished from *Jñāna*, knowledge of the divine. That is why, art and Iconography in ancient India always deeply related to the consciousness of divine beauty which undoubtedly infuse *Rasa* (sentiment), *Aditi* (infinites), *Paramātman* (supreme self) and *Anubhava* (inner experience or feelings) which are still involved to the contemporary society of India. For that reason, ancient Indian civilization always showed unity in diversity regarding the iconic features of the deities without any religious rivalry and jealousy between different Indian sects.

It is to be noted that, the glorious aspect of Indian culture and civilization tried to lead humanity ahead and elevate the level of human values which was also proved in the vast field of religious sectarian tolerance in the day to day life of ancient India. In the creation of many images of the deities from different cults, genuine attempts towards a reconciliation between the principal religious sects are illustrated. In this regard, one of the collections of Indian Museum, Kolkata, should be mentioned where it is found that the four sides of roughly squared *Śivaliṅgas* are curved the figures of Viṣṇu, Durgā-Pārvatī, Sūrya and Gaṇapati along with the central *liṅga* and this symbolizes the cult pictures of five principal sects, i.e., Vaiṣṇava, Śākta, Saura, Gāṇapatya and Śaiva. Early and late mediaeval period miniature shrines with the representations of the chief sectarian Gods of these five religious sects have been discovered in various places of Northern India, specially at Varanasi which has been the place of different Brahmanical sects from very early period. It is also to be noted that, according to our *Smṛti* text the worship of five cult deities (*pañcopāsanā* or *pañcayatanapūjā*) is one of the most important practices during every religious ceremony. This sort of mental attitude in religion, no doubt indicates the spirit of reconciliation and re-approachment between different sects. It is said that Brahmanical, Buddhist and Jain religious systems of India developed well filled pantheons and increased by the fact that free and frequent interchanges of deities inspired the artists with different innovative ideas without religious intolerance. There are so many examples such as Brahmanical deities

Sarasvatī, Lakṣmī and Śiva are to be found among the Buddhist pantheon as Prajñāpāramitā, Vasudhārā and Siṃhanāda. Pārvatī and Indra are to be found among the Jain pantheon. Brahmanical deities Tārā, Chinnamastā, Manasā are included in Mahāyāna Buddhist pantheon as Mahācīna Tārā, Vajrayoginī and Jāṅgulī respectively. A very favorite mode of representing Lakulīśa in Eastern region, especially in Orissa is to show him as Buddha, in the great miracle of Śrāvastī. He is seated on a double petalled lotus being raised up by to Nāga kings and his hands are in the *dharmacakramudrā* which indicates the amalgamation and absorption of Buddhism with Brahmanical Śaiva sect.

It has been observed that free interchanges of deities took place first at the very outset of Buddhism and Jainism as well as in the more promiscuous Tantric age and gradually this tradition influenced the Muslim spiritualists to achieve a development of their intuitive faculties through ascetic exercises, contemplation, renunciation and self-denial. In spite of the destruction and vandalism due to the Islamic invasion in India, some portions of Muslim community were influenced gradually by the essence of eternal piece and universal brotherhood (*vasudhaiva kuṭumbakam*) of our glorious civilization. Thus, Sufism spread in different parts of India through the customs and rituals of the day to day life. All these have a great impact on the art and iconography as well as the artistic narrative and socio-political life of India, our heavenly Motherland.

System of Transliteration

(Vowels)

a	ā	i	ī	u	ū	ṛ	ḷ	e	ai	o	au
अ	आ	इ	ई	उ	ऊ	ऋ	लृ	ए	ऐ	ओ	औ

aṃ	aḥ
अं	अः

(Consonants)

k	kh	g	gh	ṅ	c	ch	j	jh	ñ
क्	ख्	ग्	घ्	ङ्	च्	छ्	ज्	झ्	ञ्
ṭ	ṭh	ḍ	ḍh	ṇ	t	th	d	dh	n
ट्	ठ्	ड्	ढ्	ण्	त्	थ्	द्	ध्	न्

p	ph	b	bh	m
प्	फ्	ब्	भ्	म्

y	r	l	v	ś	ṣ	s	h
य्	र्	ल्	व्	श्	ष्	स्	ह्

Application of Transliteration

(Chapter-3)

"kautsyaśāva iti khyāto vīrasenaḥ kulākṣayāḥ/
śabdārtha-nyāya-lokajñaḥ kaviḥ pāṭaliputrakaḥ/
kṛtsnapṛthvījayārtthena rājñaiveha sahāgataḥ/
bhaktyā bhagavataśśambhorguhāmetāmakārayat/"

"कौत्सशाव इति ख्यातो वीरसेनः कुलाक्षयाः ।
शब्दार्थ-न्याय-लोकज्ञः कविः पाटलिपुत्रकः।।
कृत्स्नपृथ्वीजयाथेन राज्ञैवेह सहागतः।
भक्त्या भगवतश्शम्भोर्गुहामेतामकारयत्।।"

(Udayagiri Cave Inscription of Candragupta II)

Abbreviations

Primary Sources:

A.V.	Atharvaveda
Aṣṭā.	Aṣṭādhyāyī
Bṛ. S.	Bṛhatsaṃhitā
MBh.	Mahābhārata
Ni.	Nirukta
Rāma	Rāmāyaṇa
Ṛ.V.	Ṛgveda
T.S.	Taittirīyasaṃhitā
Gīta.	Gītagovinda
Śūnya.P.	Śūnyapurāṇa
Śuk.N.	Śukranītisāra

Some Other Terms:

P.	Page
Vol.	Volume
Aṣṭa.	Aṣṭapadī

Chapter One

Origin and Development of Indian Iconography

The term *'Iconography'* originates from the Greek word *eikōn* (image) and *graphein* (to write) which literally means — 'image writing' and the term is specially meant for worship or associated with the rituals connected with the worship of different divinities.

Iconography concerns mainly with the study of the religious figures in stones, metals, woods, terracotta, paintings or on coins or seals etc. This branch of art is not merely concerned with the studies of the content of images but it also deals with delineation of the figured sculptures, frescoes or such other objects, which are executed on different parts of the shrine mainly for decorative purposes. Thus, in its broader sense, the term iconography really signifies the interpretative aspect of the religious art of a country which becomes manifest in diverse ways. Even before the evolution of the image proper representing of the principal deity of the cult, when such a divinity is usually represented by various aniconic symbols as in the case of early Buddhism, the monuments also associated with it contain numbers of illustrative of various mythological stories connected with it. The funerary monuments of Bharhut and Sāncī contain numerous figures, sculptures, medallions and reliefs related to the religious art of India. Similarly, *ṭāṅkās* (banner paintings) of Tibet, Nepal and Central Asia show a definite religious character in this branch of knowledge. That is why Grünweden rightly said, "*the religious character, so deeply rooted in the national life of Indians has also continued the guiding principle in their art.*"

In this perspective, we can say that Iconography is the art and science of designing temples, architectural elements, sculptures and the ornamentation of religious significance as described in the literary sources of Ancient India, i.e., Vedic and Purānic literature, *Dharma*, *Artha* and *Nīti* texts and specially in the numbers of *Śilpa* texts.

Materials for the study of Indian Iconography are of two distinct kinds archaeological and literary. The primary source for the study of the Brahmanical and the Buddhist as well as *Jaina* images are archaeological in nature, which includes not only stone sculptures, terracotta figurines, bronze and metal statues, seals, coins but also Inscriptions and numismatics. The two schools of the great Indian sculpture the Gāndhāra and the Mathurā contributed a lot to the study of the Brahmanical and the Buddhist Iconography. It must be noted that sculptures and paintings *(citras)* are very useful as these images clearly indicate the social traits of the people who made an worship to them. The reliefs curved on sections of religious architecture or figures appearing on extent frescos are also very important.

A new epoch-making contribution of the Gupta period to the history of Indian architecture is the construction of temples. These temples with their architectural grandeur are something like open museums for the study of Indian images of a large number of Gods and Goddesses.

During the Pāla and the Sena periods, the unprecedented expansion of Buddhism in to the Vajrayāna sect helped to develop much more original Buddhist images, which opened up a new vista for the study of Buddhist Iconography. A large number of images, both Brahmanical as well as Buddhist were constructed in these periods particularly in Bengal and Bihar.

Two other sources, epigraphical and numismatic in character have great importance in the study of the Indian Iconography. Coins, discovered from various parts of northern India, give us a complete idea of the early iconographic types of various Gods and Goddesses engraved on them. These numismatic depictions are generally based on the actual sculptural representation. The figure of Gautama Buddha belonging to the 2nd Century C.E. is well represented in plastic form among the *Gāndhāra* sculpture and the coins of Kaniṣka clearly described by Kuṣāṇa die-cutter "*Śākyamuni Buddha*" show the great similarity between these two. Similarly, the figure of lord Śiva in the extant Gāndhāra Sculptures of 2nd-3rd Century C.E. must be compared to the coins of Kaniṣka and Huviṣka where such divinities described by the die-cutters. It must be said that the devices appearing on the earliest indigenous coins of India shade a flood of life on the symbolic representations of God and Goddesses.

Inscriptions also serve important data for the study of Iconography. Inscriptions and Epigraphical records not only inform the peculiarities of religious cults but also state the erection of shrines and construction of images of divinities to be enshrined in them. The Ghośuṇḍi Inscription of the 2nd Century B.C. refers to the erection of a *Pujāśīlaprakāra*, round the shrines of Saṅkarṣaṇa and Vāsudeva which presumably contained the images of these Gods. Many and various are the Gupta epigraphic records which refer to the creation of shrines of such divinities of Bhavānī, Kātyāyanī, Śiva, Buddha, Mahāvīra and others indicate throw a new life in the study of Iconography. The royal seals which were impressed on the copper plate records of rulers responsible for issuing those charters often contain the representation of various religious objects specially used by the kings as their respective royal insignia. For example, the imperial Gupta ruler Samudragupta who seems to have been an ardent follower of Viṣṇu used Garuḍa as his royal emblem on his charters and this is known from Allahabad Pillar Inscription "*garutmadaṅkāśvaviṣayabhukti*"[1]. It is also noted that the Garuḍa emblem was depicted on most of the gold and silver coins of the imperial Guptas. In the inscriptions of the Pāla rulers of Bengal the word "*paramasaugata*" i.e., the devout worshipper of Buddha is found. The Pāla rulers used the symbol representing the preaching of the first sermon by the master as their royal insignia. The copper plate grants of Sena kings of the Bengal bear in many cases the figure of the lord Sadāśiva, the patron deity of Senas and was utilised as the royal insignia of Sena kings. The copper plate grant of *Mahāsāmanta Śrīmad* Dommanapāla who was the

1 Sircar, D.C., *Select Inscription*, Vol.1, P- 262

local ruler of Southern Bengal contains a very beautiful outline drawing of Nārāyaṇa Viṣṇu riding on a chariot and his *vāhana,* Garuḍa on its reverse sight which show the significant iconographic details. Thus, the epigraphic records furnish scholars with interesting and significant materials for the study of Iconography.

The primary source of iconographic studies is obviously archaeological materials described above but none can minimize the importance of literary works in this respect. Literary sources have great corroborative value. The *Vedas*, the *Sūtra* texts, the epics and the *Smṛti* texts cannot be looked upon as works on Iconography, yet they contain some features of different gods and goddesses. In Ṛgveda, Indra is referred as Suśipra i.e. having beautiful cheeks and jaws, Deva Rudra as Kapardin (wairing braided coil of hair), Vāyu as Darśata (striking to the eye, beautiful). In Ṛgvedic hymns Sūrya (Sun God) traversing through the wide firmament of the sky could be easily conceived as a mythical bird having beautiful wings — *"Suparṇo garutmān"*. The Goddess Ūṣa is said to lead a white seed in a Ṛgvedic verse.[2] It is also noted that Vedic Viṣṇu, one of the constituent elements of the composite cult, God Vāsudeva-Nārāyaṇa-Viṣṇu of the epic and Purānic period is none but one of the aspects of the Sun God in the Vedic period. Thus, it must be said that early and later Vedic literature indicate the basic similarity of the Iconographic conceptions of numbers of Brahmanical deities with the anthropomorphic details. In this respect it must be said that the main sources for the study of Iconography are obviously the *Purāṇas*, the *Āgamas*, the *Tantras* and the

2 Ṛ.V., 77.7.3

Śilpaśāstras. The *Purāṇas*, like Agni, Matsya, Padma and Viṣṇu contain descriptions of different deities which are very much essential for proficiency in Brahmanical Iconography and it must be mentioned that all the Puranic texts also associate themselves prominently with one or other of the few principal sects (i.e., Vaiṣṇava, Śaiva, Śākta, Saura, Gāṇapatya) and contains elaborate details about *pratimālakṣaṇa* or *devatārcanakīrtana*, *pratiṣṭhāvidhi* (the exact method of the installation of images) and *devagṛhanirmāṇa* (construction of temples and others).

Iconographic and Iconometric texts were also allotted some place in some authoritative early Indian works on astronomy and *Nītiśāstra* of which the name of Vṛhatsaṃhitā must be mentioned. The Bṛhatsaṃhitā of Varāhamihira tells us *"deśānurūpabhūṣaṇa-veśālaṅkāramūrtibhiḥ kārya pratimalakṣaṇasaṃyuktā sannihitā briddhidā bhavati"*[3], which means that the ornamentation and clothing as well as beautification of the images should be worked out in accordance with the usage in the country in which the images are made. The Iconographic matter in Śukranītisāra[4] has also immense value in the religious art of India. Of the many and various omnibus works belonging to the category of *Smṛti* or *Dharmaśāstras* there lots of Iconographic data are found. Among them the name of Caturvargacintāmaṇi of Hemadri must be mentioned in this respect. The Vratakhaṇḍa of this work contains numerous extracts dealing with the iconographic features of a really

3 Bṛ.S., 58.29

4 Śuk.N., 4.4

formidable host of Gods and Goddesses belonging to the pantheon of different Brahmanical cults.

The *Āgamas*, the principal among which are the Aṃśumadbhedāgama, the Uttarakāmikāgama, the Suprabhedāgama, the Vaikhānasāgama contain elaborate details about the materials required for the preparation, consecration and worship of several deities.

Similarly, the *Śilpaśāstras*, the Śāktatantra and some other texts deal with one or other aspect of iconographic interest. Varāhamihira's Bṛhatsaṃhitā in this connection deserves special mention as it provides two chapters to deal with the Iconography, Iconometry and the two chapters are provided for detailed description on the installation of the images (*jīrṇoddhāra*) and the materials required for the construction of images. These parts with the commentary of Bhaṭṭotpala express the valuable data of ancient Indian Iconography. Mānasāra, a famous *Śilpa* text deals with Iconography (both Brahmanical and Buddhist deities), Iconometry and the allied arts of bronze casting and painting. There are also numbers of *Śilpa* texts like Pratimālakṣaṇa, Pratimāmāṇalakṣaṇa, Kāśyapaśilpaśāstra, Viśvakarmāvatāraśāstra, Citralakṣaṇa, Aparājitā-vāstuśāstra and the texts like Samarāṅganasūtradhāra by the king Bhoja of Dhārā (11th Century C.E.), Mānasollāsa or Abhilaṣitārthacintāmaṇi by Cālukya king Someśvaradeva (12th Century C.E.), Mayamata of Mayamuni, Śilparatna of Śrīkumāra, Devatāmūrtiprakaraṇa and Rūpamaṇḍana of Maṇḍana (15th Century C.E.) and others are also must be mentioned in this respect. The texts like Haribhaktivilāsa, Hayaśīrṣapañcarātra and Tantrasāra are also need to be mentioned where iconographic details of different deities are elaborately depicted with the *dhyānamantras*. These texts contain iconographic details of Brahmanical deities. Haribhaktivilāsa and Hayaśīrṣapañcarātra connected with Vaiṣṇavism where numbers of quotations from Agni, Matsya, Viṣṇudharmottara and other *Purāṇas* are found. Tantrasāra of Kṛṣṇānanda Āgamavāgīśa contains extensive quotations from various *Tantras* like Rudrayamala, Brahmayamala, Kubjikāmata, Śāradatilaka and others. All these contains the iconographic features of Tāntric Gods and Goddesses.

In this regard it must be mentioned that the study of Iconography or the religious art of India will be incomplete without the reference of *dhyānamantras* of numerous deities connected with the different cults. The *dhyānamantras* of Brahmanical cults express the love and adoration *(bhakti)* of a personal God and the *sādhanas* of Vajrayāna Buddhism emphasise the real unity between the God to be meditated upon and the individual meditating on him. For example, we may quote one well-known *dhyānamantra* outlines the conception of God Śiva –

"dhyāyen nityaṃ maheśaṃ rajatagirinibhaṃ cārucandrāvataṃsaṃ
ratnākalpojjvalāṅgaṃ paraśumṛgavarāvītihastaṃ prasannam |
padmāsīnaṃ samantāt stutatamamaragaṇairvyāghrakṛttiṃvasānaṃ viśvādyaṃ
viśvavījaṃ nikhilabhayaharaṃ pañcavaktraṃ trinetram ||"

which indicates the clear concept with main iconographic features of lord Śiva. With this *mantra* we may compare to a *sādhana* of Siṃhanāda Lokeśvara of Vajrayāna divinities, which shows the concept that Vajrayāna deity Simhanāda is evidently based principally on the Brahmanical God Śiva.

In this respect it has to be mentioned that a broad division can be made between the Brahmanical images of north and south India on the basis of important iconographic features so the texts also can be generally classified into two groups i.e. one followed in the North and other in the South. But it cannot be denied that sometimes texts belonging to one group showed traces of their contact with those belonging to the other, as undoubtedly varieties of images usually current in one region are occasionally found in the other places. Manḍaṇa, the famous artist of Rajasthan draws copiously from both North and South Indian sources in his works and many of his descriptions of particular images are given in the approved South Indian manner. In his Rūpamanḍaṇa we find the description of the image of Sun God does not show the well-known iconographic features of the images of the God Sūrya in the North India. Actually the image making activities attain the great impetus in the early century of Christian Era due to various causes and images belonging to different creeds came to be made in large numbers the artists entrusted with this tasks put their own experiences and experiments into writing not only for their own convenience but also for the next generations of artists and in this way a vast mass of such texts grew up gradually which were being added to from time to time.

In spite all of these it must be said that untold numbers of images of ancient and mediaeval period in marble, statuaries and architectural pieces from different places of India were destroyed by various classes of people for different purposes. But still, some of those sculptures of great iconographic interest where restored and preserved in different museums in India, which shows the glorious field of Iconographical study in ancient India.

In conclusion it must be said that the art of sculpture and painting attained an amount of perfection in ancient India which could stand comparison with what was attended in other civilized countries. In ancient India freedom for the display of thought and feeling through art constituted the very life of all art and the technique of image making also could not be treated as an exception. At that time, the Indian artists not only desired that the images of these Gods and Goddesses should be cultured beautifully, side by side they did not easily tolerate any glaring departure from the rules laid down authoritatively in the *Śastras.*

Chapter Two

Image Worship and Iconography

The origin of image worship in India has a deep-rooted past. The English word image in its primary sense has its close parallel to the Sanskrit word *vimba*, *pratikṛti* or *pratimā*. The word *pratikṛti* and *pratimā* came to denote *arccā* i.e. the objects of regular worship in course of time as Pāṇini in his Aṣṭādhyāyī refers to the *sūtra 'jīvikārthe cāpanaye'*[1]. From the commentaries of Mahābhāṣya by Patañjali (C. 2nd century B.C.E.) and the Kāṣikā by Jayāditya (C. 7th century C.E.) it can be assumed that *'jīvikārthe cāpanaye'* meant for livelihood but at the same time were not for sale. The *sūtra* may be indicated as the rule applies to the images of Gods that are made means of subsistence by the order of *Brāhmaṇas* and not by selling. Such images were undoubtedly important for the objects of worship.

According to modern research it has been suggested that the practice of image making was prevalent among the early Vedic Indo-Arians as there are so many descriptions of the divinities given in various hymns which have been indicated definite allusion to images.

In the Vedic hymns, we find some words like *naras*, i.e., men, *divo naras,* i.e., men of the sky and *nṛpeśas*, i.e., having the form of men[2] which clearly refer to the images

1 Aṣṭā., 5.3.99

2 Ṛ.V., 3.4.5

of human forms to their Gods with the sensible manners. In the Ṛgveda the description of a painted images of Rudra is found:

"sthirebhiraṅgaiḥ pururūpa ugro |
babhruḥ śukrebhiḥ pipiśe hiraṇyaiḥ ||"[3]

(With strong limbs, many formed, awful brown, he is painted with shining golden colours).

In the first *Maṇḍala* of Ṛgveda the description of Varuṇa is found:

"vibhraddrāpiṃ hiraṇyayaṃ varuṇo vasta nirṇijam | pari spaśo niṣedire ||"[4]

(wearing a golden coat of mail, he veils himself in his radiance, spies seat around him).

There are some words like *vapuḥ, tanu, rūpa* in Vedic texts used in connection with some of the Vedic Gods has particular reference to their images. In Taittirīyasaṃhitā and Atharvaveda a passage *"svayā tanvā tanumayīrayata"*[5] (with your own real body enter this concrete body clearly indicate the physical tenement of the real form of the god), i.e. one the concrete and finite and other the abstract and infinite and this theory was totally developed with the Upaniṣadic *Brahmaṇ - ātman* concept where the words *Īśa, Īśvara* and *Parameśvara* are used.

In the time of Yāska, image-worship was prevalent, at least, among the ritualists. In his Nirukta, Yāska has furnished two contradictory views on image and image-

3 Ṛ.V., 2.33.9

4 Ṛ.V., 1.25.13

5 T.S., 1.7.12, A.V., 7.33

worship. According to him, the image conception belonged to the ritualists *(yājñikas)* and not to the *Niruktakāras*. To the *yājñikas*, Gods resemble human beings in form:

"puruṣavidhāḥ syuriti ekam |"[6]

Niruktakāra also said that Gods are associated with the sort of action with which men are usually associated:

"tathābhidhānāni |"[7]

Yāskācārya also indicates the other view which say that the Gods do not resemble human beings in form:

"apuruṣavidhāḥ syuriti aparam |"[8]

because those Gods that are actually seen do not resemble human beings in form, as, for example, Agni (the Fire-God), Vāyu (the Wind-God), Āditya (the Sun-God), Pṛthivī (the Earth-Goddess), Candramas (the Moon-God) and the like.

Pāṇini, the great grammarian and philologist, mentions in one of his grammatical aphorisms, *"ive pratikṛtau"*[9] a term *'pratikṛti'*, the literal meaning of which is 'something made after the original'. It is obvious, then, that *pratikṛti* is but a reference to the divine images which were meant not for selling in the market but for making a living by procuring alms from the devotees.

In the age of the *Purāṇas*, the *Upapurāṇas*, the *Āgamas*, the *Tantras* and the *Śilpaśāstras* conception of image-making flourished to a great extent. In the Puranic

---

6 Ni., 7.6.2

7 Ni., 7.6.4

8 Ni., 7.7.1

9 Aṣṭā., 5.3.96

age, Vedic ritualism was simplified and forms of various deities like Viṣṇu, Śiva, Gaṇeśa, Sūrya, Kṛṣṇa, Durgā, Kālikā, Kārtikeya were conceived and given shapes, too, to meet the demand of the day. In the third part of the Viṣṇudharmottarapurāṇa, there is an elaborate discussion on the art of painting, icons of different deities, the art of temple building, effect of image-worship and the like and for that reason this *Purāṇa* has been rightly regarded as "a veritable encyclopaedia on Brahmanical Iconography." The valuable discussion of this chapter is no doubt the iconographic representations of different Brahmanical deities which is also the basis of the art of Indian paintings, cultures and architectures.

In the epic Rāmāyaṇa, we get mention of image-concept and image-worship.[10] In the Vanaparvan of the Mahābhārata Śālagrāma[11], aniconic form of Lord Viṣṇu in the Puṇḍarikatīrtha is found. There is also a reference to the image of Nandīśvara found in the Anuśāsanaparvan of the epic "*Nandīśvarasya mūrtiṃ tu dṛṣṭvā mucyeta kilviṣaiḥ.*"[12] The early Sanskrit literature, say for example, the Pratimānāṭaka of Bhāsa, description of human image is given also.

In this respect it must be said that in the origin and development of image worship in India the idea of *bhakti* plays the main role and for this reason some sensible objects became indispensable in different sects. The symbols and images for the various personal Gods from different sects analogically did the same sort of service as was done by

10 Rāma., 2.71.40

11 Mbh. III, 84.124

12 Mbh. XIII, 26.61

Agnideva in Vedic ritualism *(karmakāṇḍa)*. In the case of a particular sectary the image or icon or any such visible symbol of his deity was the handy medium through which he could transfer his one souled devotion, '*ekātmikā bhakti*' to his God. It is also said that the rendering of one's homage was done by various acts of worship in which images were absolutely necessary. That is why *abhigamana* or going to the temple of the particular deity with the speech, the body, and the mind centred on him, *upādāna* or collecting the materials of worship such as flowers, sandal paste, offerings *(naivedya)*, etc., *ijyā*, the very act of worshipping the *Śrīvigraha svādhyāya*, the uttering of the *mantra* to the particular cult divinities and *yoga* or meditation – all these are included in the act of *pūjā* or worship which play the special role in the history of the evolutions of the icons. Another theory regarding image worship indicates that the Hindus worshipped images mostly to concentrate the mind upon some external objects during the practice of *yoga*. The image maker fashioned images in such a manner that they would conduce to the success of the *dhyānayoga*. Many images are known where the deity himself is shown in the pose of the *yogī* immersed in the deep meditation. The images of *yogāsana* Viṣṇu, *yogadakṣiṇāmurti* of Śiva and others support this theory. In the Śāntiparvan of Mahābhārata there is an interesting passage related to Nārada's visit to the Badarikāśrama which supports such view where Nārāyaṇa himself was an object of worship and the Lord explains Nārada that he is worshiping his original *prakṛti* the source of all that is and that is to be.

The true significance and purpose of the image proper of the God is fully emphasized by the later works as 'Rāmapūrvatāpanīya', 'Jāvāladarśanopaniṣat' and 'Mahānirvāṇatantra'. These works are mainly written from the point of view of those who firmly believed in worshipping the highest principle without the aid of any media *(nirākāropāsanā)* and attitude of some of them was strictly nondualist *"śivamātmani paśyanti"*. But still, some of these texts deprecate the practice of the persons who offers their *bhakti* to their Gods through different acts of *pūjā* or worship.

It is said that a well-executed image if it followed the rules of proportion laid down in the *Śilpaśāstras* and is pleasing to the eye, invites the deity to reside in it and is particularly auspicious to its worshipper. That is why in India, iconism and aniconism existed side by side from a very early period which is also present even in modern times.

Both the Hindu and the Buddhist Iconography flourished side by side and both owed a great deal to each other. The Hinduism made of Buddha an *avatāra*, a God and so did Buddhism. Besides painting, sculpture too is a treasure house of the Hindu and the Buddhist Iconography. The oldest instances of sculpture, distinctly Hindu in character, is the *liṅga* at Guḍimallam in South India. It is supposed to belong to the period of Bharhut sculptures of the second century before Christ. Similarly, the Inscription on a Garuḍa Pillar at Besnagar in Madhya Pradesh gives clear evidence of the worship of Viṣṇu as Vāsudeva in the temples of India not later than the 2nd century B.C.

The Hindus worship images of Gods and Goddesses, *Śālagrāmas* (taken to be representative of Viṣṇu), *Bāṇaliṅgas* (representative of Śiva), *Yantras*, some special trees (viz., Aśvattha, Tulasī), holy rivers like Gaṅgā, Kāveri, Godāvarī, certain animals like cow and sepulchres of saints. Besides these, they pay homage to some local objects of their personal choice.

The Hindu images are mainly divides into two major groups- the Vaiṣṇava and the Śaiva. Pāṇini in his Aṣṭādhyāyī mentioned the *sūtra* *"vāsudevārjunābhyāṃ vun"*[13] which refers to the worshippers of God Viṣṇu. Patañjali in his Mahābhāṣya refers to a sect called the Śivabhāgavatas or devotees of Śiva who carried in their hands an iron lance as an emblem of Śiva whom they worshipped. Patañjali in his comment on Pāṇini's Sūtra (5.3.99) mentions the name of the dieties whose images were being made for worship at his time "*Sampratipūjārthaḥ*". Not only that in the early Buddhist works there we find the various kinds of worship of different deities prevailed in India especially in central and Eastern Indian at the time when Gautama Buddha preached his doctrine. Later the images of different mother Goddesses, Gaṇeśa and some other deities, which are, according to the *Purāṇas*, related to one way or another, to Viṣṇu or Śiva. One aspect of the Hindus looking at the religious objects deserves special mention. The Hindus even through the process of sanctification and deification may make any object, small and large, an object of worship but in all cases, it is not the object which is worshipped in reality, rather the object is understood to represent the deity intended to be worshipped.

The Buddhist, on the other hand, did not worship such objects as *Śālagrāmas* or *Bāṇaliṅgas*. Although in the Buddhist *Tantra*, Maṇḍala, a tantric meditation device,

---

13 Aṣṭā., 4.3.98

which is very much akin to Hindu *yantra*, has given a high position.

The sculptured images of Brahmanical cult can be classified under three major categories: *cala* (movable), *acala* (immovable) and *calācala* (movable immovable). The painted images also can be categorised under three heads: *citra*, *citrārdha* and *citrabhāṣa*. A fully sculptured image is called *vyakta* (manifest), half-represented image is called *vyaktāvyakta* (manifest and non-manifest) and an image without representation is called *avyakta* (non-manifest). The *Śālagrāmas* and *Bāṇaliṅgas* are examples of *avyakta* while the *trimūrti* in the Elephanta cave can be cited as an example of *vyaktāvyakta*.

The images, again, can be classified under two major heads depending upon their nature: the *raudra* or *ugra* and the *śānta* or *saumya* form of deities are worshiped for the attainment of something pious and chaste.

It is to be noted that our ancient sculptors have segregated sculptures into five distinct divisions: *nara*, *krura*, *āsura*, *bālā* and *kumāra* and determined five varieties of *tālas* and *mānas* for the makings of those five kinds of images *(mūrtis)* e.g. *naramūrti (daśatāla)*, *kruramūrti (dvādaśatāla)*, *āsuramūrti (ṣoḍaśatāla)*, *bālāmūrti (pañca-tāla)* and *kumāramūrti (ṣaṭtāla)*.

The sculptors, along with this have determined the measurement of one *tāla (ekatāla)* in this fashion: one-fourth (1/4th) of the fist of the sculptor is taken to be one finger and twelve fingers make one *tāla (ekatāla)*. They, thus, have ordained that the *mūrtis* Naranārāyaṇa, Rāma, Nṛsiṃha and so on be framed in the *naramūrti* or *daśatāla* fashion. Similarly, the images of Caṇḍī, Bhairava, Hayagrīva etc. be sculptured in *krura* or *dvādaśatāla* fashion; the images of Hiraṇyakaśipu, Hiraṇyākṣa, Rāvaṇa etc. be framed in the *āsura* or *sodaśa tāla* design. The images of Vaṭakṛṣṇa, Gopāla etc. be framed in the *bālā* or *pañcatāla* design and *kumāra* or *ṣaṭtāla* be used in the making of those images who have crossed their childhood days though but yet to cross adolescent stage of their life i.e., those living in between their childhood and adolescent stages of life. The sculptures of Umā, Vāmana etc. belong to this category.

Besides these five distinct categories, Indian sculptors follow another format known as *navatāla* in the making of images. According to this format known as *navatāla* the whole body of the sculpture is divided into equal nine parts and each part of the body is known as *tāla*.

In connection with the discussion of the classification of images, it is essential to discuss on different basic *bhāva* or pose. In Indian sculptures four kinds of *bhāva* or *bhaṅga* (pose) can be noticed as they are: *samabhaṅga* or *samapāda*, *ābhaṅga*, *tribhaṅga* and *atibhaṅga*.

- *samabhaṅga* or *samapāda*: In this *bhaṅga* the image stands erect on its feet without bending to either side. The sculptures of Buddha, Sūrya and Viṣṇu are structured in this technique. Here *bhaṅga* of the left and the right side of the body remain the same; only the hand-posture differs.
- *ābhaṅga* : In this *bhaṅga* the image stands or sits bending towards its left (right side of the sculptor) or right (left side of the sculptor). Mainly images of the saints are framed in this fashion.

- *tribhaṅga* : In this *bhaṅga* or technique the image stands or sits bending towards its right (left to the sculptor) like a reel or flame of fire from feet to waist; from waist to throat, towards its left (right to the sculptor), and from throat to head, towards its right again i.e., into total body of the sculpture can be seen three distinct bends.
- *atibhaṅga* : This kind of technique is practically an extension of the *tribhaṅga* technique; the only difference being that here the image is framed with some extra bends of the body. Here the body assumes the shape of a tree broken by the devastating storm. In it is seen the body from waist to head or from waist to feet scattered in the left, right, front or back of the body. This technique is used particularly to portray the devastating Śiva *(Śiva-tāṇḍava)* or fights between *devas* and *dānavas*. When the sculptors want to add more vigour and vivacity or power of dancing to the sculptures, they use this technique, which is supposed to be the most appropriate means of expressing ideas.

In the ancient texts like the Śukranītiśāra and Bṛhatsaṃhitā, *māṇa*, *parimāṇa*, nature and feature of the images are described in details. In the making of the sculptures, we can cite basic advice of the ancient sculptors:

"*sevyasevakabhāveṣu pratimālakṣaṇaṃ smṛtam*"[14]

The *lakṣaṇa*, *māna*, *parimāṇa* etc. which have been described here are associated mainly with those sculptors

14 Śuk.N., 4.259

or their mentors i.e., the founders of sculptures (or deities), whose relationships are of (objects) worshipped and worshippers or masters and servants. These kinds of images must be framed according to the strictures of the *Śāstras.* No deviation is at all entertained here.

Temples of the Hindu and the Buddhist deities are built as per specifications and instructions laid down in the *Āgamas* and the *Tantras*. Between these two texts, there is little difference. The *Āgamas* deal with twenty five subjects viz., the nature of *Brahman*, *Brahmavidyā*, creation and destruction of the world, names of different *Tantras* etc. but *Tantras* treat only seven out of twenty five subjects mentioned in *Āgamas.*

Ancient India believes in the omnipresent God who dwells in everywhere in the core of heart of the devotees and in stocks and stones. Depending upon the spiritual wisdom of the devotees the presence of God can be felt. To a *yogī*, neither an external image nor a temple is required, for, the realise the presence of the supreme *Brahman* within himself. However, those who have not yet attained this height of realization need various kinds of deities for worship and various injunctions of the *Śāstras* to abide by. Moreover, the image worship is said to bring on the worshippers rebirths and the *yogī* who aspires for freedom from bondage *(mukti)* cannot be resort to it.

The Brahmanical Gods and Goddesses and representations of various conceptions of divine attributions has been made manifest and concretised by means of speech, pictorial and sculptural representations as well as sign and symbols. All these are but mere means to bring divinity down to the level of common people and lift them to the level of sublime height of true realization.

In India there is gentle merging in iconography with image worship without any marked line of demarcation between them. Freedom for the display of thought and feeling through art constitutes the base of the aesthetic sense and the art of image making cannot be treated as an exception. Though our ancient sculptres always desired that the images of his Gods and Goddesses should be sculptured beautifully still there were also some prescribed norms and forms laid down authoritatively in the *Śāstras* which were to some extent partially followed but in spite of these it must be concluded that as the art of image making contains the freedom for the display of thought and feelings of the artists as well as worshippers the divine beauty was their ultimate goal.

Chapter Three

Iconography and Communal Harmony

Iconography is one of the essential parts of the glorious civilization of ancient India and the study of Iconography throws some interesting light on the presence of rivalry and jealousy between diverse Indian sects. The religious history of India cannot show many instances of intense hatred and violent strife between the members of rival sects as are to be found in the religious history of Europe and other countries. In this connection it must be noted that different icons illustrated genuine attempts towards a reconciliation between the principal rival sects. The images of Harihara, Ardhanārīśvara and such others can be distinctly shown to bear traces of such different mental approach to religious problems. There are several sculptures in Indian museum, Kolkata which emphasise such peculiarity. On the four sides of roughly squares *Śivaliṅgas* are carved the figures of Viṣṇu, Durgā, Pārvatī, Sūrya and Gaṇapati, along with the central *liṅga* that symbolises the cult pictures of the five religious sects i.e. Vaiṣṇava, Śākta, Śaiva, Saura and Gāṇapatya.

The words *pañcopāsana, pañcāyatanapujā*, written in *Smṛti* texts of Manu and Yājñavalkya indicate the five cult deities and the spirit of reconciliation as well as rapprochement between the different sects also shows such noble attitude in religion. In this connection it must be noted that in the Brahmanical Hindu icons there, lots of Buddhist Iconic motives are found. In Orissa a very favourite mode of representing Lakulīśaḥ (one of the famous preachers of Śaiva cult) is to show him as Buddha in the great miracle of Śrāvasti as he is seated on a double petalled lotus being raised up by two Nāga kings and his hands are in the *Dharmacakramudrā.*

From the 12th major rock edict of Aśoka the religious tolerance of the king is clearly announced:

"no ca tu tathā dānaṃ vā pūjāṃ vā devānāṃ priyaḥ manyate yathā - sārabriddhiḥ syāt sarvapārṣadānām .... ātmapārṣadapūjā va parapārṣadagarhanaṃ vā no syāt aprakaraṇe .... pūjayitavyā eva ca tu parapārṣadāḥ tena tena ākāreṇa / evaṃ kurvan ātmapārṣadaṃ vardhayati parapārṣadam api ca upakaroti/"[1]

The Maurya king himself was the follower of Buddhism but always encouraged the friendly relation among different sectarian communities. According to him no one should praise the own religion and hate the other sect only. On the other hand, everybody should give up their hatred and preach love and friendship.

Imperial Gupta rulers belonged to Vaiṣṇavism by religion but the people of different religious sects easily performed their day today life without any obstacles. Udayagiri Cave Inscription of Candragupta II, Sānci Stone Inscription, Meharauli Iron Pillar Inscriptions and so other show the generosity of Gupta rulers related to religious

---

1 Sircar, D.C., *Select Inscriptions*, Vol.1, P- 32

tolerance. That is why apart from Vaiṣṇava cult, Śaivas, Śāktas, Sauras, Bauddhas, Jainas all were welcomed to live peacefully during the Gupta reign with their religious belief.

There are several evidences furnished by the monuments of both Śiva and Viṣṇu temples side by side erected by the devotees during Gupta period. Among them the Śiva temple at Bhumra in Nagod, Pārvati temple at Nachnakuthara in Ajaygarh, a temple of Śiva at Khoh in Nagod are the important monuments which revealed that being the followers of Vaiṣṇava cult, Gupta monarchs also patronised the worshipers of Śiva. From Mathurā Pillar Inscription of Candragupta II, (dated in the Gupta era 61) it is recorded that Uditācārya, a Śaiva *Guru* (teacher) installed two *liṅga* images known as Kapileśvara and Upamiteśvara in the Gurvāyatana. Uditācārya, designated as *Ārya,* meaning respectable probably was the fourth in succession from Parāśara and tenth from Kuśika according to the Śaiva tradition. In the Sānci Inscription there are other teachers like Upamitra and Kapila who are called as *Bhāgavatas* i.e., persons who attend the rank of divinity. It is also interesting to note that the term, *Bhāgavata* was applied for the eminent preceptors in Gupta period and also this term could not be applied to a particular sect of religion.

The undated Udayagiri Cave Inscription of Candragupta II records the consecration of the cave temple to God Śambhu, one of the appellations of God Śiva. The excavation of this temple was at Udayagiri which was done by Vīrasena, one of the ministers of Candragupta II and was also descendent of a renowned family Kautsa (*Kautsaśāva*) of the city Pāṭaliputra. Vīrasena must have sought the permission and assent of the king to excavate a temple in honour of God Śambhu (Śiva). The most interesting fact is that Candragupta II being a Vaiṣṇava came to Udayagiri with his minister Vīrasena and perhaps saw the temple by himself:

"Kautsaśāva iti khyāto vīrasenaḥ kulākṣayāḥ/
śabdārtha-nyāya-lokajñaḥ kaviḥ pāṭaliputrakaḥ/
kṛtsnapṛthvījayārtthena rājñaiveha sahāgataḥ/ bhaktyā
bhagavataśśambhorguhāmetāmakārayat/"[2]

In this connection it must be mentioned that the Ardhanārīśvara form of Śiva in the Brahmanical Iconography of Mathurā is well-known during the Gupta period and its Iconographic wealth shows the spirit of religious tolerance. In the Sanakānīka cave at Udayagiri near Bhilsa (excavated early in the 5th century C.E.) there the figure of Mahiṣāsuramardinī with four arms is found next to the image of Viṣṇu. It is also noted that the Udayagiri cave contents also the images of the seven divine mothers. The icons of the Goddess Ambikā represented on the coins of Candragupta I and II shows that the Śakti cult was also popular during Gupta period. Fleet in his 'Gupta Inscriptions' mentioned to Inscription No. XVII where an independent data points to the prevalence of the cult of divine mothers. The Inscription was issued by king Viśvavarman, one of the feudatory Lord under the Gupta emperor Kumāragupta who with his minister is set to have built a temple for the divine mothers.

Mandasor Stone Inscription of Viśvavarman and Bandhuvarman during the rule of Kumāragupta I contains

2 Sircar, D.C., *Select Inscriptions*, Vol.1, P- 279

an interesting datum about the solar form of worship where the opening lines begin thus:

"yo'bhyudyatā-kṛtsnaṃ
yaśca gabhastibhiḥ pravṛsritaiḥ puṣṇāti lokatrayam/
gandharvāmara-siddha-kinnara-
naraissaṃstūyate'bhyutthito/
bhaktebhyaśca dadāti yo'bhilaṣitaṃ tasmai savitre
namaḥ/"[3]

May that Sun protect you who is worshipped by the hosts of Gods for the sake of existence and by the Siddhas who wish for the supernatural powers and by ascetics, entirely given over to abstract meditation and having worldly attractions well under control, who wish for the final liberation of the soul and with devotions by saints, practicing strict penances, (who wish to become) able to counteract curses, and who is the cause of destruction and commencing again of the Universe.

It is known from the record of the Chinese traveller I-tsing that the temple of Mṛgaśikhāvanam was built by Śrigupta, exclusively for worshiped by people from China. Most probably this Śrigupta was the founder of the Gupta dynasty and it would appear that it was a Buddhist shrine which was tolerated by the early Gupta monarchs. During the reign of Samudragupta, it is also noted that the Ceylon Buddhists enjoyed the privilege of being votaries of the Buddha in the land of his birth. There is also a story related to the king Meghavarṇa of Ceylon, who despatched certain monks to the Gupta monarch Samudragupta to seek permission to erect a monastery at Buddhagayā. Not only that Meghvarṇa gave lots of gifts to Samudragupta and

3 Sircar, D.C., *Select Inscriptions*, Vol.1, P- 299

obtained perpetual sanction for the Ceylonese pilgrims to reside at Buddhagayā. From the Sānci pillar inscription of Candragupta II it is known that Sānci continued to be a centre of attraction for Buddhists not only in India but also from abroad (China, Tibet etc.). It is also noted that the famous Chinese pilgrim Fa-Hien visited India during the reign of Candragupta II. From the Mankuwar Stone Image Inscription during the reign of Kumāragupta I it has been known that Buddhamitra a Buddhist monk installed an image of lord Buddha. All these evidences show that Buddhism continued to flourished during the reign of Gupta rulers who did not interfere with the fate or its tenets. That is why Buddhagayā, Sānci, Mathurā and Sāranātha seem to have been flourishing centres of Buddhism during Gupta period.

During the reign of Kumāragupta I, an Inscription at Mathurā records that the images of the *Jaina tīrthaṅkaras* were set up only after the necessary permission was obtained from there *Ācārya* (preceptor) who had the power to sanctioned such dedication. Udayagiri Cave Inscription of Kumāragupta I also records how a devotee named Śankara installed an image of the *Jaina tīrthaṅkara* Pārśvanātha. From the Kahaum stone Pillar Inscription of Skandagupta, it has been informed that five images of *Jaina tirthankaras* were installed. Thus, it may be said that Gupta emperors of the 4th and 5th Century A.D. were perfectly tolerant towards Jainism.

It is also said that the royal patronage of a religion is not a bad index of its general influence and popularity. In Bengal the Candras, the Pālas, the Varmans, the Sena kings and other individual rulers like Kāntideva and

Raṇavaṅkamalla were the followers of different religious sects. But in spite of the existence of these religious sects there was no sectarian jealousy or exclusiveness. From the famous Rājataraṅgiṇī of Kalhaṇa we come to know that in Kashmir, the rulers (from *Kali* era 653 – Christian era 14th century) set up numbers of temples and erected numbers of icons related to the Śaiva, Vaisṇava and Śākta cult as well as the many Buddhist monasteries and *Jaina* temples. Thus, it is realised that like the other parts of India the Bengal region also proved the religious tolerance in day today life and there are so many references in contemporary epigraphs regarding this matter which cannot be ignored. Pāla kings were the followers of Buddhism, Dharmapāla and Vigrahapāla III are given credit in official records for maintaining the orthodox social order of casts. Nārāyaṇapāla himself built an endowed a temple of Śiva. He not only attended sacrificial ceremony of his Brahmin ministers but also reverently put the sacrificial water on his head. The chief queen of Madanapāla regarded it as meritorious to hear the recital of Mahābhārata. Queen Prabhāvatī of the king Devakhaḍga set up an image of Caṇḍī. In Paharpur Copper Plate, it is found that the Śaiva king Vainyagupta endowed the Buddhist monastery and a Brahmin with his wife made a pious gift of land to a *Jainavihāra*. These instances show respect and reverence for others creed and there are also certain facts which indicate even a more intimate association between different religious sects. Buddhist Dhanadatta married a Śaiva princess and eagerly knew the Rāmāyaṇa, the Mahābhārata and *Purāṇas*. There are also some interesting cases in which a king openly declares his devotion to more than one religious faith. King Vaidyadeva styles himself both Paramamāheśvara and Paramavaiṣṇava. King Śrimad Dommanapāla, the follower of Śaiva Māheśvara sect paid his respect to *Bhagavān* Nārāyaṇa. In the Copper plate grants of Visvarupasena and Keśavasena the royal seal attached to plates bears the representation of Sadāśiva and is actually called *Sadāśiva mudrā* in the body of the Inscription. Though the Sena kings are the followers of Vaiṣṇava cults they are given the title Paramasaura. It seems that the later Sena kings not only professed the two great faiths followed by their forefathers but also added new one, the Saura cult. Such spirit characterises the religious life of Bengal even today where almost every Hindu performs a worship of Nārāyaṇa, Lakṣmī, Śiva, Durgā, Kārtika, Sūrya and other Gods and Goddesses with equal zeal and venerations.

While both Vaiṣṇavism and Śaivism derived their strength and inspiration from the magnificent temple from the great community of *Brāhmaṇas* distinguished for their religious zeal and learning the main strongholds of the Buddhists were the numerous monasteries. From the records of Hiuen-tsang it is known that there was 17 Buddhist *Vihāras* accommodating 8000 monks and no less than 300 *deva* temples in Bengal region. Not only that it has been also known from different epigraphical evidences and from the accounts of Tibetan writers that the numbers of Buddhists monasteries, monks and temples increased with subsequent times up to 13th Century C.E.. Bengal studied with Hindu temples and Buddhist monasteries and was also the home of the body of learned *Brāhmaṇas* and Buddhist monks whose livelihood was made easy and secured by private or royal charity. I-tsing gave detailed account of Buddhist monastery of Tāmralipta in Bengal where he himself lived for some time. It is also said that the *Brāhmaṇas* were also inspired by an equally high ideal is abandonly proves the work of Bhavadevadatta, Halāyudha and Vallālasena.

In this respect, it is said that a popular religious cult, named Dharma cult developed in Eastern region specially in Bengal (Western Bengal) out of the admixture of Buddhism with Brahmanical ideas and practices. Though, archaeological investigations have revealed that ideas and practices similar to those of the Dharma cult are to be found also in Mayurbhanj and its vicinities of Orissa and South-Western part of Bengal. Dharma cult owes many of its elements to that form of Vajrayāna Buddhism. Not only that, the process of assimilating the local indigenous practices of Dharma cult show the same tendency as it is found in the religious practices of Tantric Buddhism and in few Buddhist texts this has been discussed. Regarding *Dharmapūjāvidhāna* of the Dharma cult we may compare more particularly one well known compendium of the religious practices of Vajrayāna Buddhism, i.e., *Kriyāsaṃgraha*. In this religious practise the offering to the Goddess Hāritī consists of fish, blood of animals, meat along with other articles which resembles the performance of fire-sacrifice and the sacrifice of animals to the Goddesses in Brahmanical Tantric process. It is also interesting to note that the stone images of Dharmaṭhākura (*Dharmaśilā*) are of the shape of a tortoise which has similarity with the miniature forms of the Nepalese Buddhist representation of the *stūpa* along with the five Bodhisattvas inscribed on them. According to M.M. Haraprasad Shastri, the tortoise is well known mythological figure in the Puranic and Tantric literature and Buddhistic interpretation of it since unwarranted. In this connection it is interesting to note that in Gītagovinda of Jayadeva, the famous poet and ardent follower of *bhaktivāda* described Kurma as the second incarnation and Buddha as the ninth incarnation of lord Viṣṇu[4]. According to the literature of Dharma cult Lord Viṣṇu was born as Jagannātha who is none but lord Buddha and is settled on the sea coast where he has relieved the whole world by distributing to all irrespective of cast creed his *prasāda*.

Image worship occupied an acknowledged and important place in the religious life of all over India from Pre Christian and early post Christian period till the introduction of various sectarian religions in which *bhakti* or loving adoration of the one personal God by his devotees from the fundamental elements. In ancient Bengal it is found that the images of Gaṇapati and Kārtikeya ought to be studied along with the Śaiva icons, figures of Gaṇapati, Brahmā, Śiva, Viṣṇu and Kārtikeya are also associated with the icon of Durgā and from Dakṣiṇa Mohammadpur (modern Tripura) such an unique two handed image of goddess Durgā of late 11th – early 12th Century C.E.. is preserved in the Indian Museum which shows the religious harmony among the different sectarian cults. In Bengal the presence of the Gods of five main sectarian cults are often found on the top of the black slabs on so many Śakti images which shows undoubtedly the Mahāyāna influence. It is realised that in Indian religion the element of *bhakti* and *pujā* is associated intimately with every sectarian cult and the religious tolerance is evolved from this. That is why

4 Gīta., 1.1(aṣṭa.).9

there was a little evidence of rivalry and jealousy between diverse Indian sects.

The glorious religious history of India also influences the Muslim spiritualists who attempt to achieve a development of their intuitive faculties through ascetic exercises, contemplation, renunciation and self-denial. Though there was a mass vandalism and destruction due to the Islamic invasion in India, the land of eternal peace and universal brotherhood, still gradually Hindu mystic traditions show a new way to inculcate and understanding among different groups within the Muslim community and the evolution and development of Sufism was firmly established in India from the 11th century C.E. to the beginning of 16th century C.E.. From the 11th Century C.E. onwards in India the contacts between Sufi sages and Hindu *Yogīs* became more frequent and meaningful and there was an interaction between different schools of Indian philosophy. Al-Bīrūnī (11th Century C.E.) informed an unquestionable authority on comparative religions. He also notes Sufi parallels in the Yogasūtra of Patañjali with himself translated into Arabic. He also mentions similarities with Sāṃkhya philosophies and with the Bhagavadgītā. It is interesting to note that the views of Patañjali and those of Sufism concerning meditation of the truth, i.e. 'Supreme God' is reflected in Sufi theory. Regarding the Sufi doctrine of love as being a total obsession with God, Al-Bīrūnī coats interesting parallels from the Bhagavadgītā. Thus, gradually the Hindu mystical songs were recited at different gatherings and became popular at all Sufi centres throughout India. The Vaiṣṇavite influence of Sufism occurred mainly through the devotional poetry. This form of Hinduism involved the worship of Viṣṇu or the Nārāyaṇa who was generally adored in the form of two of his ten incarnations, Rāma and Kṛṣṇa and also in the form of worship of their consorts. The panentheistic mysticism of the Upaniṣads, the devotional mysticism mainly in the Vaiṣṇavite line and Sahajiyā movements of Bengal no doubt influence Sufism. This will account for the speedy growth of Sufiistic faith in the large portions of India which is deeply related to the evolution of the minor religious sects like the Bāuls of Bengal and Santa poets of Northern and Western India. Similarly, the Nātha and Siddha *Yogīs* of Śaiva sect spread from Punjab to Bengal lived in forests, wondered in towns and also established permanent monasteries. Mixed with the Muslim followers sectional *Yogīs* also popularised syncretic beliefs. The literature of Buddhist Sahajiyā, Vaiṣṇava Sahajiyā, Nirguṇa school of Northern and Western India and also the literatures of Sufi poets were adopted by Nātha *Yogīs* who employed or the Yogic practices for the attainment of immortality. In this respect, it must be said that the development of Dharma cult in Western and South-Western Bengal was gradually assimilated into the cognate religious system among the Hindus and the Muslims. After the Islam invasion of Bengal (circa 12th-13th century C.E.) Muslim began gradually to settle in the land and to exert political, religious and cultural influence on the people. It is also said that the follower of the Dharma cult with their monotheistic belief in the formless God could easily have friendly turns with the Muslim community who had the same belief and this seems to be palpable influence of the Muslims in the description of *Dharmapūjāvidhāna.* This has also been observed related to the customs of sacrificing goat or duck or pigeon before Dharmaṭhākura by cutting their throat in a particular manner which is peculiarly a Muslim custom. It is to be noted that in connection with the worship of *Dharma* or the accessory ceremony the gates or *toraṇa* invariably begins with the description of the western direction and also attached to the Moon depicted as *Koṭāla* of the western direction which is very much similar with the testimony to the Muslim influence. In Śūnyapuraṇa of Rāmāi *Paṇḍita* the description of *Dharmapūjāvidhāna* indicates this custom.[5]

It is also interesting to note that the process of offering food along with milk, wheat and fruits in *Satyanārāyaṇapūjāvidhi* in Bengal is very much similar to the process of sacrificing food made with milk, wheat etc. to Muslim saints, *Pīra-phakira* of the Muslim community. Thus, it is found that in some places of Bengal, a similarity is found in day to day religious customs of Hindu and Muslim community. The literature of mediaeval Bengal shows these significant similarities. It is also interesting to note that in the Dharmamaṅgala literature Dharma revealed himself as a Muslim (*Yavana avatāra*) in the place, a village named Jajpura in Hoogly district — "*jājapurer dehārā bandiva ekaman | jeikhāne avatār haila yavan ||*"[6]

During the reign of Husain Shah in Bengal (1493-1538 C.E.) the spread of communal harmony has lots of instances. The Bengal became the land of peace, justice and religious tolerance as he had a number of high-ranked officers like Gopinātha Basu, Mukundadāsa, Keśava Chatri,

5 Śūnya.P., Dharmapūjāvidhāna, P-215.

6 Ms. Entitled Dharmer vandanā, P - 1(B) (CU no. 2470) as mentioned in *Obscure Religious Cults* by Shashibhusan Das Gupta, P-266.

Gaura Mallika and others. The famous Vaiṣṇava sages, Rūpa and Sanātana Gosvāmi who in their previous life held the high position in the administrative system of Husain Shah. Being a Muslim ruler he was yet free from the rank intolerance which mars the annals of many Muslim kings of Northern India. By his patronage the earliest translation of Mahābhārata in Bengal was written by Parameśvara. During his reign Śrī Caitanya Mahāprabhu mesmerised the region with Peace and brotherhood as well as religious tolerance.

In the 10th and 11th Centuries Vaiṣṇavism was revived by the great philosopher Rāmānuja (founder of *Viśiṣṭādvaitavedānta* school) and others who emphasized devotion through image worship and simple rituals. In the meantime, a new dimension was added to Vaiṣṇavite devotionalism by Nimbārka and his contemporary poet Jayadeva of Bengal during 11th Century C.E. which played an important role amongst the many emerging *bhakti* cults. Later these *bhakti* cults were developed into *Acintyabhedābhedatatva* (incomprehensible dualistic monism) by Śrī Caitanya Mahāprabhu of Bengal to express the relationship between God and the soul. All these influenced a lot on Sufism and also made a deep impact on *Bāul* movement. Thus, from the interaction between the Hindu mystic tradition and Sufism gradually during 14th-15th C.E spread a new dimension of communal harmony in different regions of India like Bengal, Punjab and also in the Southern part of India.

It is also noted that during the reign of Alauddin Hussain Shah, Bengal was quite free from racial and religious factiousness and the credit for this undoubtedly went to the peaceful reign of Hussain Shah. He not only appointed high officers from Hindus but also put them in charge of highly confidential work that was certainly something more than mere diplomatic expediency. His literary appreciation was extended in an increasing degree to Bengali literature and with Mālādhara Basu, Vijayagupta and others. Parameśvara the earliest Bengali translator of the Mahābhārata became famous by his patronage. He was yet free from the rank in tolerance and some of the Vaiṣṇava writers ascribed to him a belief in the incarnation of Śrī Caitanya Mahāprabhu to whom he undoubtedly showed great respect.

In conclusion it must be said that the intense religiosity characterised the people all over India which is proved by the nature, scope and volume of not only the extensive religious literature but also the image worship as well as Iconography of contemporary period. It is also said that the beginnings of many of folk religions exercised considerable influence over the mass of people in Bengal as well as the other parts of India during the mediaeval period, by which the religious tolerance and communal harmony was no doubt partially established.

Chapter Four

Indian Iconography: A Comparative Study on the Basis of Religious Harmony and Tolerance

Through the analytical research of Indian Iconography, it should be realised that there are common similarities between the Brahmanical, the Buddhist and the Jain deities. Even the iconic features of Satyapīra of rural Muslim community in Bengal is influenced by lord Nārāyaṇa (Viṣṇu) i.e., Satyanārāyaṇa and this is a unique example of religious tolerance. The pantheons of different communities and religious sects in India are found to have glorified the antiquities of Indian civilization.

Comparison between Brahmanical and Buddhist Deities

It is found that a number of Brahmanical deities resemble to the deities of the Mahāyāna Buddhist pantheons. That is why Goddess Sarasvatī and Buddhist counterpart Prajñāpāramitā, Goddess Chinnamastā and her counterpart Vajrayoginī, Goddess Tārā of Brahmanical Śākta cult with her counterpart Tārādevī of Mahāyānī Buddhist pantheon, Goddess Manasā and her counterpart Jāṅgulī, Goddess Śitalā and her counterpart Parṇaśavarī,

Lord Śiva and his counterpart Siṃhanāda, Goddess Lakṣmī and her counterpart Vasudhārā, Goddess Ṣaṣṭhi and her counterpart Hāritī have some common iconic features according to Purānic texts and Buddhist Sādhanamālā.

Sarasvatī and Prajñāpāramitā

All over India Sarasvatī, the Goddess of transcendental knowledge has a paramount importance in terms of her popularity and wide appeal amongst the Gods and Goddesses of Brahmanical pantheon. According to the Viṣṇudharmottarapurāṇa Goddess Sarasvatī has four arms holding the *pustaka* and *akṣmālā* in her right hands and the *vīṇā* and the *kamaṇḍalu* in left hands. Sometimes a *padma* is seen in place of the *kamaṇḍalu* in one of the left hands and the *vyākhyāna mudrā* in the right hand instead of the *vīṇā*. Sometime the white swan is seen with the deity.

In the Mahāyāna Buddhist sect the Goddess Prajñāpāramitā is regarded as the mother of perfect wisdom. She is envisioned most often as golden in colour and alternately as white. She appears with either two or four arms. Her hands are typically brought together at her heart in a teaching gesture known as *vyākhyānamudrā*. Her upraised left hand displays a manuscript and the upraised right hand bears a rosary. The lotuses blossom above her shoulders and support a pair of perfection of wisdom scriptures.

Idol of Goddess Sarasvatī, Konark Natya Mandir, Orissa

Idol of Goddess Prajñāparamitā, Sinhasari Temple, East Java, Indonesia, 13th Century C.E.

Chinnamastā and Vajryoginī

Hindu Goddess Chinnamastā is the most awe-inspiring form of the Daśamahāvidyas. According to the Tantric scriptures Goddess Chinnamastā has radiant of million Suns. In her left hand she holds her severed head drinking blood coming out of her severed neck. She has dishevelled hair, she is decked with garlands made of human skulls and bones, she carries a *kartṛ* in her right hand and is standing in *Pratyalīḍha* posture. She is accompanied by two companions Dākinī in the left and Varṇinī in the right.

Buddhist Mahāyāna deity Vajrayoginī is one of the prime emanated forms of Ratnasambhava. Four *Sādhanas* in the Sādhanamāla describe her forms which are three in number and are two distinct types, very different from each other. In one case she has severed head carrying it in her hand and in second type is the form with intact head. The severed head form is yellow in complexion. The Goddess holds her severed head in her left hand and the *kartṛ* in her right hand. She is bare bodied and is accompanied by two *yoginīs*, the black complexion Vajravarṇanī in the left and the yellow complexion Vajravairocanī in the right. In this regard the name of Buddhist Vajrayānī deity Chinnamuṇḍā must be noted. She is described as severed headed Goddess in Vajrayāna Buddhism. Chinnamuṇḍā along with the two yoginīs is also compared with Hindu Goddess Chinnamastā and in the context of *kuṇḍalinī yoga* Vajrayānī deity Chinnamuṇḍā is compared to her perfection stage of *yoga*, i.e., *utpannakrama*, known in Buddhist terminology.

Sculpture of Goddess Chinnamastā, Carved at Chintapurni Temple Gate, Himachal Pradesh

Portrait of Goddess Vajrayoginī in a Tibetan Thanka Painting

Comparison between Goddess Tārā, Tantric Deity and Tārā Devī of Mahāyānī Pantheon

In Brahmanical tradition Goddess Tārā is known as supreme Goddess Mahādevī and is addressed as Tārā and Tārinī and is also known as one who saves her devotees from all the troubles of life.

Goddess Tārā is one of the most important *Devī* of Daśamahāvidyās with an outpouring of devotional theologies to Mahādevī as Lalitā of Śrīvidyā Tārā. Tārā is one of the most important forms of supreme mother Jaganmātā, Ādyāśakti. The supremacy of Goddess Tārā in Brahmanical as well as Tantric cult has a deep influence on Buddhist Mahāyānī (Vajrayānī) pantheon where she is worshiped as universal saviour who nurtures, assists and protects all seekers on the spiritual path.

The iconographic features of Brahmanical Tārā with Mahāyānī Buddhist deity Tārā is quite similar to some extent. She has two arms; the right hand shows *Varadamudrā* and there is a lotus in her left hand. Among the images of sixty-four *yoginīs* in the Yoginī temple of Hirapur, Orissa, there the idol of *yoginī* Tārā is also found with four hands and in standing posture on tortoise. It must be noted in this respect that in Buddhist text Sādhanamālā, there are the descriptions of four-armed Dhanada Tārā who rides on animal.

Idol of Goddess Tārā

Idol of Buddhist Goddess Tārā, circa 14th century C.E., Nepal

Idol of Goddess Tārā in 64 yoginīs, Hirapur, Orissa

Lakṣmī and Vasudhārā

The iconographic representation of the Brahmanical Goddess Lakṣmī is found in different *Śilpi* texts and also in different *dhyānamantras*. She is known as the Goddess abandons wealth, fortune and beauty. She has golden yellow colour and decked with various kinds of ornaments. She has two arms and the common attributes placed in her hands are a lotus (*padma*), a conch shell (*śaṅkha*), a pot of nectar (*amṛtaghaṭa*) *and* a wood-apple (*vilvaphala*). In some of the sculptures she has four arms also. Some of her hands are held in *Varada* and *Abhayamudrā* and she is seated on a lotus.

In the Vajrayāna Buddhist pantheon Vasudhārā is known as a Goddess of fortune and wealth. From Sādhanamālā and different manuscripts it is found that Goddess Vasudhārā has two arms and bears the image of *dhyānībuddha* Ratnasambhava on her crown. She is yellow in colour and has two arms. Her right-hand displays *Varadamudrā* and she holds in her left hand the sheaf of grain (*dhānyamañjarī*). Some images of Vasudhārā also include a vessel brimming with jewels, positioned beneath her right hand to collect the treasure that pours forth.

It is to be noted that like Brahmanical and Buddhist pantheons, the image worship of Goddess Lakṣmī is also popular in Jain temples. Number of images (both sculptures and paintings) of Śrīlakṣmī, Gajalakṣmī are found in different Jain temples and Palm leaf manuscripts.

Idol of Goddess Lakṣmī, Kashmir, 6th Century C.E.

Idol of Goddess Vasudhārā, Nepal, 14th Century C.E.

Miniatue of the Goddess Mahalakṣmī illustrated in Palm leaf manuscript of Ogha Niryukti
(Collected in Jain Grantha Bhandar, Baroda, Gujarat)

Manasā and Jāṅgulī

Manasā is the Hindu folk Goddess for protection from snake- bites. Basically, Manasā is worshipped in rural Bengal but different Brahmanical scriptures like Brahmavaivartapurāṇa, Devībhāgavata, Mahābhārata describe her place in higher level. According to Devībhāgavata her colour is as white as *campaka* flower and she is decked with different valuable ornaments along with the snakes. She has a sacred thread made of serpents.

Mahāyāna Buddhist Goddess Jāṅgulī is widely worshipped and respected amongst the Buddhists as a Goddess who curses snake-bite and even prevents it. Four *Sādhanas* in the Sādhanamālā mention different forms of Jāṅgulī. She is white in complexion, four armed and one faced. She is adorned in white ornaments of pearls and white serpents. She plays the *vīṇā* with two primary hands, holds the white snake in second left hand and shows the *Abhayamudrā* with the second right hand. In another variety, the Goddess has three faces, six arms and her complexion is yellow. Her right face has blue colour and the colour of her left face is white. In her three right hands she holds *khaḍga*, *vajra* and *bāṇa*. In her three left-hands she carries *pāśa*, *viṣapuṣpa* and *kārmuka*. She is rested upon the expanded hood of the serpent and also adorned with valuable ornaments and snakes.

Sculpture of Goddess Manasā during the reign of Pāla Kings in Bengal, circa 10th Century C.E.

Portrait of Goddess Jāṅgulī, Tibet, 15th Century C.E.

Śītalā and Parṇaśavarī

Goddess Śītalā is one of the prime non-Vedic and non-puranic popular diety. Though she is generally worshipped in rural Bengal during the spring season when small pox, cholera break out but it can be said that the amalgamation between the Arians and non-Arians might help her introduction to the Hindu pantheon. From different *dhyānas* of Goddess Śītalā, it is found that she is a white-complexioned, bare bodied Goddess. She is decked with all sorts of golden ornaments. She has three eyes and two hands of which the right one holds a broom-stick and the left one holds the pitcher full of water. she is accompanied by two consorts Jvarāsura and Raktāvalī.

Buddhist Goddess Parṇaśavarī is effective in preventing outbreaks of epidemics in assuring safety to the terror stricken. According to Sādhanamālā she is of yellow complexion with three faces, three eyes and six arms. She wears a garment of leaves and adorned all kinds of ornaments. She holds *vajraparaśu* and the *śara* in her right three hands and *tarjanipāśa*, *parṇapicchikā* and *dhanu* in her left three hands. Her *jaṭāmukuṭa* is decorated with flower and the image of Akṣabhya.

Portrait of Goddess Śitalā in Kalighat Paṭa Paintaing

Bronze Sculpture of Goddess Parṇaśavarī from Tibet

Ṣaṣṭhī and Hārītī

The idol worship of the Goddess Ṣaṣṭhī was not popular in Brahmanical religion previously. Gradually, she became the sixth part of the pre-mordial nature (*ādi prakṛti*) according to the Puranic literature like Brahmavaivartapurāṇa, Devībhāgavatapurāṇa and Nāradapurāṇa. She was a popular deity of the Kuṣāṇa period. She is revered as a child bearer and child protector and in the rural Bengal Goddess Ṣaṣṭhi is also whorshipped as child protector still now. According to the *dhyāna mantra* the Goddess has golden complexion with two arms and she is wearing fine clothes with valuable ornaments. She is accompanied with children and cats. It is also said that Goddess Ṣaṣṭhī is worshipped in various ways till the age twelve years after the birth of a child. Sometimes it is seen that Goddess Ṣaṣṭhī is imagined in the paintings on the earthenware or on the rocks.

Mahāyānī Buddhist Goddess Hārītī is known as the protector of child as well as childcare. According to Mahāvastu and other Buddhist texts Hārītī is also considered as the Goddess of fertility and healing. In the Sādhanamālā the iconic features of Hārītī are depicted as the symbol of motherhood. Consider a 3rd century statue that exhibits the level of artistry and exemplifies the Gāndhāran vision of Hārītī. The divine mother is seated on a throne in the frontal *Pralamba-pāda* pose with her knees spread and feet firmly planted on small dais. She is gracefully ornamented with dangling earrings, a torque, a heavy neckless, bracelets and anklets. She is accompanied with eight children and she cradles an infant to her breast. The other children perch on her shoulders and sport at her feet in playful attitudes.

Portrait of Goddess Ṣaṣṭhī in Kalighat Paṭa Painting

Sculpture of Goddess Hārītī of Kuṣāṇa Period, Gandharan Region, circa 3rd Century C.E.

Śiva and Siṃhanāda

According to Brahmanical sect, lord Śiva is known as the supreme God and the representative of supreme power along with Brahmā and Viṣṇu (*Trideva*). Lord Śiva is said to be an omniscient *yogī* (*Ādiyogī*). He has Pre-Vedic roots and the figure of Śiva evolved as an amalgamation of Vedic and Non-Vedic deities including Rudra (Rudrādhyāya of Śuklayajurveda).

The well-known iconographic features of lord Śiva is of two-armed (four armed also), three-eyes, white complexioned, wearing tiger skin with trident, snake and tambourine in his hands which is quite similar with Buddhist Mahayānī deity Siṃhanāda. In Buddhist Sādhanamāla text the image of Siṃhanāda (Lokeśvara) is described as white complexion with three eyes, having no ornaments, clad in tiger skin with trident, serpent and lotus bowl.

Statue of Lord Śiva

Image of God Siṃhanāda in Pao-hsiang Lou Pantheon, Peiping

The religious life in India is marked about the time of 7th -13th Century C.E. by a spirit of catholicity and mutual respect and understanding which is hardly compatible with a deliberate persecution on sectarian grounds. In this respect Buddhism exhibits this tendency and Mahāyāna as well as Vajrayāna Buddhist mysticism gave rise to new schools of Śaktism and Śaivism on the one hand and certain forms of popular religion on the other. Both of which became popular throughout Eastern India.

In this connection it must be said that in spite of different religious sects side by side there is no sectarian jealousy or exclusiveness. That is why Vaiṣṇavism, Śaivism and Śaktism derived their strength and inspiration from the magnificent temples and the great communities of Brāhmaṇas distinguished for their religious zeal, learning. This is proved by some epigraphic references. From the Inscription of Vaidyadeva it is found that Vaidyadeva styles himself both Paramamāheśvara and Paramavaiṣṇava. Deopara Inscription of Vijayasena shows the influence of Śaivism and Vaiṣṇavism during the reign of Sena kings.

Actually, religious tolerance is found throughout India among different sects and which is also proved through iconographical studies. The idol of Ardhanārīśvara shows the intimate association between Śaivism and Śaktism as well as the idol of Kṛṣṇakālī proves the interrelation between Vaiṣṇavism and Śaktism. It is also to be noted that from the image of *catuṣṣaṣṭhī yoginī* temple, Hirapur, Orissa, the amalgamation and interrelation with Śākta and Gāṇapatya cult, Śākta and Vaiṣṇava, Śaiva and Śākta are strongly proved. Not only that, interrelation between Śaktism in Brahmanical sect and Jainism is also beautifully shaped through the images which are included in the section of Illustration, plate no. 4 to 7.

Sculpture of Ardhanārīśvara, Khajuraho Temple of Chandella Dynasty, Chatarpur District, Madhyapradesh, circa 10th Century C.E.

Sculpture of Ardhanārīśvara, Elephanta Cave, Maharashtra, circa 5th-6th century C.E.

Śivaliṃga, the emblame of conjugation of Śiva and Śakti (Śaiva and Śākta cult)

Idol of Kṛṣṇakālī
(Assimilation of Vaiṣṇava and Śākta cult)

Idol of Goddess Vaiṣṇavī on Garuḍa in 64 Yoginīs,
Hirapur, Orissa
(Amalgamation of Vaiṣṇava and Śākta cult)

Another interesting point is that the Iconography of Goddess Bhavatāriṇī in a temple situated in Nabadwip, Nadia district of West Bengal strikingly resembles with the idol of Gaṇapati. It is also noted that in the sixty-four Yoginī temple, Hirapur, Orissa, the image of *yoginī* Vināyakī is very much similar to lord Vināyaka or Gaṇapati. May be, she is worshiped as the *Śakti* of lord Vināyaka which indicates the assimilation of Gāṇapatya and Śākta cult.

Idol of Lord Gaṇapati

Idol of Goddesss Bhavatāriṇī, Pora Ma Tala, Nabadwip

Idol of Goddess Vināyakī, Cherianad Temple, Kerala 13th century C.E.

Idol of Goddess Vināyakī in 64 Yoginīs Hirapur, Orissa

Gaṅgā and Jhulelal

Goddess Gaṅgā in Brahmanical concept is the personification of the holiest river Gaṅgā of India. The deity is worshiped for decades as the Goddess of purification and forgiveness known by names as Sureśvarī, Bhagavatī and other. As per her iconographic feature she is a fare and beautiful deity adorned with various ornaments, riding on a divine animal, Makara. It is interesting to note that the iconic features of Goddess Gaṅgā is quite similar to folkloric deity Jhulelal worshiped by Sindhi community of Sindh, modern Pakistan, who also is riding on Makara on the river Indus.

It is also to be noted that Jhulelal is worshiped by both Sindhi Hindus and Muslims which indicates the excellence of communal harmony between Hindu and Muslim community in North-Western India.

Idol of Goddess Gaṅgā

Idol of God Jhulelal

It is interesting to note that during Muslim period in Bengal (i.e. 12th-17th century C.E.) mixing of socio-cultural rights and rituals gradually grew up. The Vaiṣṇavite influence on Sufism made itself felt mainly through its devotional poetry and also some socio-religious festivals. Thus, the worship of Satyanārāyaṇa and Satyapīra spread over rural Bengal from 17th century C.E both in Hindu and Muslim community.

Sculpture of Lord Viṣṇu, Made of Blackstone, Karnataka, India, circa 1200-1300 Century C.E. (Preserved in the Asian Art Museum, San Francisco)

Image of Satyapīra
May be imagined according to the description of Devotional Poetry (pāñcāli)

Though there is no specific form of Satyapīra, still in the devotional poetry (*Pāñcālī*), iconographical descriptions of Satyanārāyaṇa and Satyapīra are found:

কহেন্ বৈদিকেরে ফকীরের বেশে ॥
জটাজূট ভস্ম প্রলেপাদি গাত্র ।
গলে শঙ্খ গাঁথা ধরা বাস মাত্র ॥
মুখে চাপদাড়ী খেলাতেং স্বরূপ ।
করে দিব্য খুন্তী শিরে লাল টোপ ॥

জনার্দ্দন্ যাঁহাকে বলো দেবতেশ ।
তিনী সত্যনারায়ণাংশে প্রকাশ ॥
হিঁদূতে বলে সত্যনারায়ণো তায়্ ।
তিনী সত্যপীর্ ভাই্ জবন্জাতিতে কয়্ ॥

সমক্ষে স্বচক্ষে দেখো সত্য সে পীর্ ॥
ইহা সব্ ব'লে বিষ্ণুরূপী সমক্ষে ।
দাঁড়ালেন্ জনার্দ্দন্ দেখে সে স্বচক্ষে ॥
মহাশঙ্খচক্রো গদাপদ্ম হস্তে ।
শিরে দিব্য চূড়া গরুড়্ বাহনেতে ॥
বসন্ শুভ্র পীতাম্বরেতে বুঝা যায়্ ।

Ghatak,Durgaprasad, SatyanārāyaṇerPāñcālī, Tarkaratna,Jadabeswar(ed.), Ghosal, Prabhaschandra(pub.), Raṅgapur Sahityapariṣat-kāryālaya, Raṅgapur, 1321 Vaṅgābda.

Janārdana, the one who helps all people, the one is worshipped by all Gods, and He is immersed within Lord Satyanārāyaṇa. Hindus worship Him as Satyanārāyaṇa whereas Muslims worship Him as Satyapīra.

If you are fortunate enough and Satyapīra appears in front of your eyes you will be awed and blessed the same way as if Lord Viṣṇu made an appearance.

When Lord Viṣṇu appears in front of His devotees, He is seen holding an enormous Conch Shell i.e Śaṅkha, a Cakra, a Gadā and a Padma (lotus flower) too. A sacred halo can be seen, peaked around His head. His attires are in white and is seen carried by Garuḍa on its back. Whereas Satyapīra disguised as a hermit appears in front of a Brahmin with His unkempt and dead locker hair, His body smeared in ashes and His face covered in beard. He can be seen dressed in a loose cloak, a red fez on His head, a conch shell hanging around his neck and a divine handheld tool in his hands.

Throughout the large forest area of South Bengal there the worship of Vanabibi and Dakṣiṇarāya is very popular to both Hindu and Muslim communities as these two deities protect the people from tiger and other forest animals. The iconographic features of Vanabibi resembles with the Goddess Jagaddhātri as well as Lakṣmī and Dakṣiṇarāya with Kārtikeya and it is seen almost everywhere that both deities are seated on tiger.

Idol of Vanabibi in Sundarban Area of South Bengal

Another Idol of Vanabibi with the Idol of Dakṣiṇarāya in Sundarban Area of South Bengal

Idol of Dakṣiṇarāya in Sundarban Area of South Bengal

Another form of the idol of Dakṣiṇarāya is found in same region.

This idol of Dakṣiṇarāya is an excellent example of communal harmony in Iconography as the dress and Iconic features of the deity show a meaningful mixture of the Hindu and Muslim community.

In conclusion it must be said that in Bengal and almost all over in India the existence of different religious sects is frequently found and there was a little example of sectarian jealousy and exclusiveness. On the other hand, there was several instances which show respect and reverence for others' creed, certain facts indicate even a more intimate association between different religious sects.

Conclusion

The intensive and historical as well as sociological study of Indian Iconography totally proves that religious practices are always connected with the vast field of Iconography. The stalwarts in this subject, Professor Jitendra Nath Banerjea in his famous work, *The Development of Hindu Iconography* rightly mentioned the remark of Grünwedel, "The religious character so deeply routed in the national life of the Indian races, has also continued the guiding principle in their art." It is also said that the ever-increasing pantheon of different cults is always ready to illustrate the iconographic representation through various transformations. But, in this respect it must be noted that rivalry and sectarian jealousy was almost absent in the noble culture and civilization of ancient India. According to the glorious concept of Indian civilization the omnipresent God, who is the father of the Universe, appears to reside in everything as much in the loving heart of the devotees as in stalks and stones. To a saint (*ṛṣi* or *yogin*) who has realized the Supreme God within himself, there is no need of divine image of worship but to those who have not attend this height of realization, various physical and mental moods of worship are prescribed and rules of various kinds are laid down in relation to conduct. That is why, the sectarian jealousy was not so prominent in ancient India and gradually different sectarian cults derived their strength and inspiration from such noble ideology for their religious zeal, learning and scholarship. It has been noticed that the beginnings of many of folk religions also exercised considerable influence over the contemporary society from early to medieval period in India.

Illustrations

Plate No. 1

Gold Coin of Samudragupta with Garuḍa Pillar
(Preserved in the British Museum)

Plate No. 2

Bhitari Silver Seal with Garuḍa Emblem of Kumāragupta II

Plate No. 3

Sculpture of Three Supreme Gods, Elephanta Cave, Maharashtra, circa 5th -6th century C.E.

Plate No. 4

Idol of Vārāhī in 64 Yoginīs Hirapur, Orissa

Plate No. 5

Idol of Nārasiṃhī in 64 Yoginīs Hirapur, Orissa

Plate No. 6

Idol of Yakṣinī in 64 Yoginīs Hirapur, Orissa

Plate No. 7

An Idol of Jain Yakṣinī

Plate No. 8

(a) अव्यक्तमेक(म्*) (।*)

(b) मुहम्मद(:*) अ-

(c) वतार(:*) (।*) नृप-

(d) ति(:*) महमुद (:*) (।।*)[2]

Texts, found as inscribed on some silver coins of Sultan Mahmud (Hijri 418, 1018 C.E.)

Printed in Sircar, Dines Chandra, Select Inscription, Vol. II, MLBD Pvt. Ltd., 1983

Here, Sultan Muhammad is described as *avatāra* like lord Viṣṇu.

Plate No. 9

Gold Coin of Muhammad Bin Sam with Emblem of Goddess Lakṣmī

Plate No. 10

1. [श्री]म[द]-[ह*]-
2. [मी]र-मह[म*]-
3. [द]-सा[म]

(श्री·मद्धम्मीर[4]-मुहम्मदः साम[-पुत्र]:)

Texts, found as inscribed on some gold coins of Muhammad Bin Sam (circa 12th- 13th century C.E.)

Printed in Sircar, Dines Chandra, Select Inscription, Vol. II, MLBD Pvt. Ltd., 1983

The first side of the coin there is a presentation of Goddess Lakṣmī.

Plate No. 11

The First Side of Muhammad Bin Sam's Coin with the Emblem of Śiva's bull and trident

Plate No. 12

श्री-महमद-साम (श्री-मुहम्मदः साम-पुत्रः)

Texts, found as inscribed on the first side of some billon coins of Muhammad Bin Sam (circa 13th century C.E.)

Printed in Sircar, Dines Chandra, Select Inscription, Vol. II, MLBD Pvt. Ltd., 1983

On the first side of this coin, Śiva's bull to left, Śiva's *triśūla* or trident on rump are inscribed.

Plate No. 13

The First Side of the Coin of Iltutmish with the Emblem of Śiva's bull and trident

श्रसवरी स्त्री-समसीरण देवे[3] (आसावरी श्री-शमसुद्दीनदेवः)

Texts, found as inscribed on some billon coins of Iltutmish, (circa 13th century C.E.)

Printed in Sircar, Dines Chandra, Select Inscription, Vol. II, MLBD Pvt. Ltd., 1983

On the first side of this coin, there are Śiva's bull to left, trident on hind quarter. The legend on this coin appears to indicate that Sultan Iltutmish came to the very Āsāvarī (Sanskrit Āśāpurī), Goddess who fulfils devotee's desire, is very significant in the socio-cultural history of Sultani period.

Bibliography

Primary Sources

Abhilaṣitārthacintāmaṇi of Someśvaradeva (*Mānasollāsa*), (Part I), R. Shamasastri (ed.), Oriental Library Publishers, Mysore: 1926.

Agni purāṇa, Panchanan Tarkaratna (ed.), Navabharati Publishers, Kolkata, First Edition: 1999.

Aitareyabrāhmaṇa, M. Hang (Eng. Translation), Bharatiya Publishing House, Delhi: 1976.

Amarakoṣa, Hargovind Shastri (ed.), Chaukhamba Sanskrit Series, Varanasi: 1979.

Aṅguttaranikāya, E.M.Hare (Eng. Translation), Pali Text Society, London : 1924.

Āpastambadharmasūtra (with Commentary *Ujjalā* of Śrī Haradattamishra), Dr. Umesh Chandra Pandeya (ed.), Chaukhamba Sanskrit Series, Varanasi: 1969.

Arthaśāstra, R. Shamasastri (ed. & translted), Mysore, Fifth Edition: 1956.

Aṣṭādhyāyī, S.N.Basu (ed. & translted), Motilal Banarsidass Publishers Pvt. Ltd., Delhi: 1962.

Atharvaveda, Bijanbihari Goswami (ed. & transltd.), Haraf, Kolkata, First Published: October, 1978.

Atharvavedasaṃhitā, W.T. Whitney (Eng. Translation), Motilal Banarsidass Publishers Pvt. Ltd., Delhi: 1962.

Atṛsaṃhitā, Panchanan Tarkaratna (ed.), Vangavasi, Kalikata : 1296 (Vaṅgābda).

Baudhāyanadharmasūtra (with *Vivaraṇa* Commentary of Govindsvamī), Dr. Umesh Chandra Pandeya (ed.), Chaukhamba Sanskrit Series, Varanasi: 1972.

Bhāgavatpurāṇa, J.L. Shastri (ed. & translated), Motilal Banarsidass Publishers Pvt. Ltd., Delhi: 1987.

Brahmavaivartapurāṇa, Panchanan Tarkaratna (ed.), Navabharat Publishers, Kolkata, First Published: Bengali Month of Jyaiṣṭha, 1931 (Vaṅgābda).

Bṛhatsaṃhitā, M.Ramkrishna Bhat (ed.), Part II, Motilal Banarsidass Publishers Pvt. Ltd., Delhi/Varanasi/ Patna/Madras, First Published : 1982, Second Revised Edition: 1987.

Bṛhatsaṃhitā, A. Jha (ed. & translated), Chaukhamba Vidya Bhavan, Varanasi: 1969.

Bṛhatsaṃhitā of Varāhamihira, (Vol. 1 & 2), Kern Cospar Hendrik Johan (text ed.), Iyer Chidambaram N (translated), Jugnu Shrikrishna (ed.), Second Edition, Parimal Publication, Delhi: 2018.

Gītagovinda of Jayadeva with comm. Rasikapriya of King Kumbha and Rasamanjari of Mahamahopadhyaya Shankara Mishra, Mangesh Ramakrishna Telang and Wasudev Laxuman Pansikar (ed.), Nirṇaya-sāgara Press, Bombay: 1899.

(*The*) *Kauṭilīya Arthaśāstra,* Vol. I, II & III, R.P.Kangle (ed. & translated), University of Bombay, 1965-1972, Reprint, Motilal Banarsidass Publishers, Delhi: 2003.

Kāmandakīya-nītisāra, M.L.Dutt (Eng. Translation), Chaukhamba Sanskrit Series, Varanasi: 1979.

Mahābhārata, K.M.Ganguli (ed. & translated), Kolkata, First Published: 1926.

Mahābhāratam (with the commentary *Bhāratabhāvadīpa* of Śrīmannilakaṇṭha), Udyogaparvan, Haridasa Siddhantavagish (ed. & translated), Vishavani Prakashani, Kalikata: 1345 (Vaṅgābda).

Mahābhāratam, Bhīṣmaparvan, Haridasa Siddhantabagish (ed. & translated), Siddhanta Vidyalaya, Kalikata: 1343 (Vaṅgābda).

Mahābhāratam, Karṇaparvan, Haridasa Siddhantabagish (ed. & translated), Siddhanta Vidyalaya, Kalikata: 1346 (Vaṅgābda).

Mahābhāratam Anuśāsanaparvan, Haridasa Siddhantavagish (ed. & translated), Siddhanta Vidyalaya, Kalikata: 1342 (Vaṅgābda).

Majjhimanikāya (3 vols.), V. Trenckner and Lord Chalmers, PTS, London: 1888-99.

Manusaṃhitā, Upendranath Mukhopadhyay (ed.), Vasumati Sahityamandir, Kalikata: 1336 (Vaṅgābda).

Manusmṛti, Rajvira Sastri, Arsh Sahitya Prachara Trust, Deli: 1985.

Manusaṃhitā with Kulluka's Commentary (ch. VII), Prof. Satyendranath Sen (ed. & translated), Chattopadhyay Brothers, Fourth Edition: 1959.

Matsyapurāṇa (Vol. II), Sri Ramasharma Acarya (ed.), Sanskriti Samsthana, Khajakutub, Bairely, U.P.: 1970.

Markaṇḍeyapurāṇa, Panchanan Tarkaratna (ed.), Navabharat Publishers, Kolkata, First Navabharat Edition: Bengali Month of Āṣāḍha, 1390 (Vaṅgābda), Reprint: 1405 (Vaṅgābda).

Matsyapurāṇa, Panchanan Tarkaratna (ed.), Navabharat Publishers, Kolkata, First Published: Bengali Month of Phālguna, 1316 (Vaṅgābda), Reprint: 1406 (Vaṅgābda).

Nirukta, Amareswar Thakur (ed.), Part - I & III, University of Calcutta, Kolkata, First Edition: 1955, Reprint: 2003.

Rāmāyaṇa, Vasudeva Lakshman Sastri (ed.), Indological Book House, Delhi, First Published: 1983.

Rājataraṅgiṇī of Kalhaṇa (Vol. I, II & III), Aurel Stein (ed. & translated), Motilal Banarsidass, First Edition, Bombay: 1892-1900; Reprint, Delhi: 1961-2003.

Ṛgvedasaṃhitā, Ralph T.H. Griffith (Eng. Translation), Motilal Banarsidass Publishers, Delhi: 1973.

Ṛgvedasaṃhitā, Ramesh Chandra Dutta (compiled), Nimai Chandra Pal (ed.), Sadesh, Kolkata, Reprint: 2007.

Śrautapāṭha, Pattabhiram Shastri (ed.), Vol-I, University of Calcutta, Kolkata, First Edition: April 1942, Third Edition: May 1967.

Śukranītisāra (Śukrācārya) (with commentary by Pandit Jīvānanda Vidyāsāgara), Prof. Manabendu Banerjee (ed.), Prof. Binay Kumar Sarkar (translated), Sadesh, Kolkata, First Combined Edition: 2007.

Śūṇyapurāṇa of Rāmai Paṇḍita, Shri Nagendranath Basu (ed.), Vaṅgīya Sāhitya Pariṣad, Cornwallis Street (Kalikātā): 1314 (Vaṅgābda).

Viṣṇudharmottarapurāṇa, Kshemaraj Shrikrishnadas (ed.), Nag Publishers, Delhi: 1985.

Viṣṇusmṛti in First Volume of Āryaśāstra, Shri Kalipada Tarkacarya and Shri Srijiva Bhattacharya, Nyayatirtha (ed.), Shri Sitaramavaidika Mahavidyalaya, Kalikata: 1370 (Vaṅgābda).

Yājñavalkyasmṛti (with the commentary of Vijñānesvara), Narayanarama Acarya Kavyatirtha (ed.), Nirnayasagar Mudranalaya, Kashi: 1944.

Secondary Sources

Agarwal, P.K.: *Goddesses of Ancient India,* Abhinav Publication, New Delhi: 1993.

Allan, J.: *Catalogue of the Coins of Gupta Dynasties and of Śaśāṅka, King of Gauḍa*, British Museum, London:1914.

Altekar, A.S.: *The Coinage of the Gupta Empire and its Imitations,* Numismatic Society of India, Varanasi:1957.

Banerjea, Jitendra Nath: *The Development of Hindu Iconography,* University of Calcutta, Kolkata, First Edition: 1941, Second Edition: 1956.

Bhandarkar, D.R.: *Aśoka,* Fourth Edition, University of Calcutta: 1969.

Bhattacharya, Benoytosh: *The Indian Buddhist Iconography,* Firma K.L.M., Kolkata, First Edition: 1924, Second Edition: 1958, Reprint: January, 1968.

Cunningham, A.: *The Stūpa of Bhārhut,* Indological Book House, Varanasi: 1966.

Das, A.C.: *Ṛgvedic India,* Calcutta, 1927.

Das Gupta, Shashibhusan: *Obscure Religious Cults*, Firma KLM Private Limited, Seventh Edition, Kolkata:1946.

Dikshitar, Ramachandra, V.R.: *The Gupta Polity,* Reprint, Motilal Banarsidass, New Delhi: 1993.

Ghosh, Niranjan: *Concept And Iconography of The Goddesses of Abundance And Fortune In Three Religions of India,* Calcutta, First Published: 26th December, 1979.

Griffith, J.: *The Paintings in the Buddhist Cave Temple in Ajanta*, Secretary of State for India in Council, London: 1896.

Kinsely, David: *Hindu Goddesses: Vision of the Feminine in the Hindu Religious Tradition,* Motilal Banarsidass, Delhi: 1987.

Majumdar, R.C.: *The History of Bengal* (*Vol. 1*), Reprint, BR Publishing Corporation, New Delhi: 2003.

Mishra, P.K.: *Studies In Hindu And Buddhist Art,* Abhinav Publication: 1999.

Mukherjee, B.N.: *Kushāṇa Coins of the Land of the Five Rivers,* Indian Museum, Kokata:2004.

Mukherjee, Radhakumud: *Aśoka,* First Publication, Motilal Banarsidass, Delhi: 2004.

Nagar, Shanti Lal: *The Cult of Vinayaka*, Intellectual Publishing House, First Edition, New Delhi:1992.

Pereira, Jose: *Monolithic Jinas* (*The Iconography of Jain Temples of Elora*), Motilal Banarsidass, Delhi: 1977.

Rao, Gopinath, T.A.: *Elements of Hindu Iconography,* Motilal Banarsidass, Delhi: 1985.

Rizvi, Abbas; Athar, Saiyid: *A History of Sufism in India* (*Vol. 1*), *Fourth Edition,* Munshiram Manoharlal Publication Pvt. Ltd., New Delhi: 2012.

Roy Choudhury, Mohanlal: *The Din-i-Ilahi or the Religion of Akbar,* Fourth Edition, Munshiram Manoharlal Publication Pvt. Ltd., New Delhi: 1997.

Sarkar, Jadunath: *History of Bengal* (*Vol. 2*), Second Reprint, BR Publishing Corporation, New Delhi: 2004.

Sircar, D.C.: *Select Inscriptions Bearing on Indian History and Civilization* (*Vol.- I*), V.K. Publishing House, New Delhi:1942.

Sircar, D.C.: *Select Inscriptions Bearing on Indian History and Civilization* (*Vol.- II*), Motilal Banarsidass, New Delhi:1983.

Shaw, Miranda: *Buddhist Goddesses of India,* Originally Published by Princeton University Press, USA: 2007, First Indian Edition Published by Munshiram Manoharlal Publication Pvt. Ltd., New Delhi: 2007.

Website Searched

www.pixels.com

https://en.wikipedia.org/wiki/Prajnaparamita

www.pinterest.com

https://wiki/Ardhanariswara

https://himalayanbuddhistart.wordpress.com

Index

A

Ābhaṅga 19
Abhayamudrā 49, 53
abhigamana 15
Abhilaṣitārthacintāmaṇi 7
abstract 12, 27
acala 18
Ācārya 28
accessory 35
Acintyabhedābhedatatva 36
action 13
ādi prakṛti 59
Āditya 13
Ādiyogī 62
administrative system 36
adolescent 19
adoration 8, 32
adorned 53, 56, 75
Ādyāśakti 45
aesthetic 22
Āgamas 5, 7, 13, 21
Agni 6, 8, 13
Agnideva 15
Ajaygarh 25
Akṣabhya 56
akṣamālā 39
Alauddin Hussain Shah 36
Al-Bīrūnī 33
Allahabad Pillar Inscription 4
allusion 11
alms 13
amalgamation 56, 62, 65
amṛtaghaṭa 49
Aṃśumadbhedāgama 7
Ambikā 26
ancient 2, 7, 9, 10, 18, 20, 21, 22, 23, 32, 87
aniconic 1, 14
aniconism 16
animal/s 17, 31, 45, 75, 82
anklets 59
anthropomorphic 5
antiquities 38
Aparājitāvāstuśāstra 7
aphorisms 13
Arabic 33
arccā 11
archaeological 2, 5, 31
architectural 2, 3, 9
architecture/s 2, 14
ardent 4, 32
Ardhanārīśvara 23, 26, 65
Arians 56
art/s 10, 14, 22
artistry 59

artists 9, 10, 22
Artha 2
Ārya 25
Asia 2
ascetic 33
Aśoka 24
assimilation 71
association 29, 65, 86
Aṣṭādhyāyī 11, 17
Astronomy 6
āsura 18, 19
āsuramūrti 18
Aśvattha 17
Atharvaveda 12
atibhaṅga 19, 20
attainment 18, 34
attitude/s 16, 24, 59
attributes 49
attributions 21
auspicious 16
authoritatively/authoritative 6, 10, 22
authority 33
Avatāra 16
Avyakta 18
awe-inspiring 42

B

bāla 18, 19
bālamūrti 18
bāṇa 53
*Bāṇaliṅga*s 16, 17, 18
Bandhuvarman 26
banner painting 2
bare bodied 42, 56
Bauddha/s 25
Bāul 34, 36
beauty 22, 49
Bengal 3, 4, 28, 29, 30, 31, 32, 34, 35, 36, 37, 38, 53, 56, 59, 71, 77, 82, 86
Bengali 37
Besnagar 16
Bhagavadgītā 33
Bhagavān 30
Bhāgavata/s 25
Bhagavatī 75
Bhairava 19
bhakti 8, 14, 16, 32, 36
bhaktivāda 32
bhaṅga 19, 20
Bharhut 1, 16
Bhāsa 14
Bhaṭṭotpala 7
bhāva 19
Bhavadevadatta 31
Bhavānī 4
Bhavatāriṇī 71
Bhilsa 26
Bhoja 7
Bhumra 25
Bihar 3
black 32, 42
blood 31, 42
blossom 39
blue 53
Bodhisattva/s 31

Bondage 21
bones 42
bracelets 59
Brahmā 32, 62
Brahman 21
Brāhmaṇa/s 11, 30, 31, 65
Brahmaṇ-ātman 12
Brahmanical 2, 3, 5, 6, 7, 8, 9, 14, 18, 21, 24, 26, 31, 38, 39, 45, 49, 53, 59, 62, 65, 75
Brahmavaivartapurāṇa 53, 59
Brahmavidyā 21
Brahmayāmala 8
Brahmin 29
Bṛhatsaṃhitā 6, 7, 20
Bronze 2, 7
broom-stick 56
brotherhood 36
Buddha 3, 4, 16, 19, 24, 27, 28, 32
Buddhagayā 27, 28
Buddhamitra 28
Buddhism 1, 3, 8, 16, 24, 28, 29, 31, 42, 65
Buddhist 2, 3, 7, 16, 17, 21, 24, 27, 28, 29, 30, 31, 34, 38, 39, 42, 45, 49, 53, 56, 59, 62, 65
Buddhistic 32

C

cakra 81
cala 18
calācala 18
Cālukya 7
campaka 53
Caṇḍī 19, 29
Candra/s 28
Candragupta I 26
Candragupta II 24, 25, 26, 28
Candramas 13
cast/s 29, 32
catholicity 65
categorised 18
cats 59
Caturvargacintāmaṇi 6
catuṣṣaṣṭhī 65
central 17, 23
Central Asia 2
century/ies 3, 4, 7, 9, 11, 16, 26, 28, 29, 30, 32, 33, 34, 36, 59, 65, 77
ceremony 29, 35
Ceylon 27
Ceylonese 28
chariot 5
charters 4
Chatri 36
cheeks 5
child bearer 59
childcare 59
child protector 59
children 59
China 27, 28
Chinese 27, 28
Chinnamastā 38, 42
Chinnamuṇḍā 42
cholera 56
Christ 16
Christian Era 9, 29, 32

Citra 2, 18
citrabhāsa 18
Citralakṣaṇa 7
citrārdha 18
civilization 23, 38, 87
clad 62
classification 19
cognate 34
coin/s 1, 2, 3, 4, 26, 100
colour 39, 49, 53
commentary 7
communal harmony 35, 36, 37, 75
communities 24, 38, 65, 82
community 30, 33, 34, 35, 38, 75, 77
compendium 31
complexion 42, 53, 56, 59, 62
conch shell 49, 81
concrete 12
consorts 34, 56
constituent 5
construction 2, 4, 6, 7
contemporary 29, 36, 37, 88
contemplation 33
copper plate 4, 29, 30
corroborative 5
counterpart 38, 39
countries 10, 23
cow 17
cradles 59
creation 4, 21
creed 9, 29, 32, 86
crown 49
cult/s 1, 4, 5, 7, 8, 15, 18, 23, 24, 25, 26, 29, 30, 31, 32, 34, 36, 38, 45, 65, 71, 87
culture/s 14, 87
curses 53
custom/s 34, 35

D

Dākinī 42
Dakṣiṇ Mohammadpur 32
Dakṣiṇarāya 82, 85
dānavas 20
Darśata 5
Daśamahāvidyās 42, 45
daśatāla 18
datum 27
decades 75
decked 42, 49, 53, 56
deities 5, 6, 7, 8, 14, 17, 18, 21, 23, 38, 56, 62, 82
deity 1, 4, 9, 15, 16, 17, 39, 42, 45, 59, 62, 75
delineation 1
Deopara 65
descendent 25
destruction 21, 33
Deva 5, 30
devagṛhanirmāṇa 6
Devakhaḍga 29
devas 20
Devatāmūrtiprakaraṇa 7
devatārcanakīrtana 6
Devī 45
Devībhāgavata 53
Devībhāgavatapurāṇa 59

devices 3
devotee/s 13, 17, 21, 25, 28, 32, 45, 81, 87, 100
devotion 15, 27, 29, 36
devotional 33, 34, 45, 77, 80
devotionalism 36
devotional poetry 33, 77, 80
devout 4
Dhanadā Tārā 45
Dhanadatta 29
dhanu 56
dhānyamañjarī 49
Dhārā 7
Dharma 2, 31, 32, 34, 35
Dharmacakramudrā 24
Dharmamaṅgala 35
Dharmapāla 29
Dharmapūjāvidhāna 31, 34, 35
Dharmaśāstra / s 6
Dharmaśilā 31
Dharmathākura 31, 34
*dhyāna*s 56
*Dhyānamantra*s 8, 49, 59
dhyānayoga 15
Dhyānībuddha 49
die-cutter 3
dishevelled hair 42
distinct/ly 2, 16, 18, 19, 20, 23, 42
diverse 1, 23, 33
divine 13, 21, 22, 26, 59, 75, 81, 87
Divinities 1, 3, 4, 8, 11, 15
divinity 1, 21, 25
divonaras 11
doctrine 17
duck 34
Durgā 14, 23, 30, 32
dvādaśatāla 19
dynasty 27

E

earthenware 59
Earth Goddess 13
Eastern 17, 31
Eastern India 65
eikon 1
ekatāla 18
ekātmikā bhakti 15
elements 2, 5, 31, 32
Elephanta cave 18
emanated 42
emblem 4, 17
emperor/s 26, 28
emphasise 8, 23
encyclopaedia 14
English 11
enshrined 4
envisioned 39
epic/s 5, 14
epidemics 56
epigraphic 4, 5, 65
epigraphical 3, 30
epigraphs 29
epoch making 2
Europe 23
evolutions 1, 15, 33, 34
excellence 75

F

factiousness 37
Fa-Hien 28
fare 75
fashion 18, 19
feature/s 5, 6, 8, 9, 20, 38, 39, 45, 59, 62, 75, 82
feet 19, 20, 59
fertility 59
feudatory 26
figure/s 1, 2, 3, 4, 23, 26, 31, 32, 62
fine clothes 59
finite 12
Fire God 13
fire-sacrifice 31
firmament 5
fish 31
Fleet 26
flowers 15, 53, 56, 81
folk 37, 53, 88
folkloric 75
forest 34, 82
forgiveness 75
forth 49
fortune 49
freedom 10, 21, 22
fresco/s 1, 2
frequent/ly 33, 86
friendship 24
fruit/s 35
fundamental 32
funerary 1

G

Gadā 81
Gajalakṣmī 49
Gaṇapati 23, 32, 71
Gāṇapatya 6, 23, 65, 71
Gāndhāra 2, 3
Gandharan 59
Gaṇeśa 14, 17
Gaṅgā 17, 75
garlands 42
garment 56
Garuḍa 4, 5, 81
Garuḍa Pillar 16
Gaura Mallika 36
Gautama Buddha 3, 17
generosity 24
Ghośuṇḍi Inscription 4
Gītagovinda 32
glaring 10
glorious 10, 23, 33, 87
goal 22
goat 34
Godāvarī 17
God/s 3, 4, 5, 7, 8, 9, 10, 11, 12, 13, 14, 16, 17, 21, 22, 25, 26, 27, 30, 32, 33, 34, 36, 39, 62, 81
Goddesses 3, 5, 7, 8, 10, 16, 17, 21, 22, 26, 30, 31, 32, 38, 39, 42, 45, 49, 53, 56, 59, 71, 75, 82
golden 12, 39, 49, 56, 59
golden yellow 49
Gopāla 19

Gopinātha Basu 35
grammarian 13
grandeur 3
grant/s 4, 30
graphein 1
Greek 1
grounds 65
Grünweden 2
Guḍimallam 16
Gupta 2, 4, 24, 25, 26, 27, 28
Gupta era 25
Gupta Inscriptions 26
Guru 25
Gurvāyatana 25

H

Halāyudha 31
Haribhaktivilāsa 7, 8
Harihara 23
Hāritī 31, 39, 59
harmony 32
hatred 23, 24
Hayagrīva 19
Hayaśīrṣapañcarātra 7, 8
head/s 18, 20, 29, 42, 81
healing 59
Hemādri 6
hermit 81
Hindu/s 15, 16, 17, 18, 21, 24, 30, 33, 34, 35, 36, 37, 42, 53, 56, 75, 77, 81, 82
Hinduism 16, 34
Hiraṇyakaśipu 19
Hiraṇyākṣa 18
Hirapur 45, 65, 71
history 2, 15, 23, 33, 100
Hiuen-tsang 30
homage 15, 17
Hoogly 35
Hussain Shah 35, 36, 37
Huviṣka 3
hymns 5, 11

I

Icon/s 14, 15, 24, 26, 29, 32
Iconic 38, 39, 59, 75
Iconic motives 24
Iconographic 3, 5, 6, 7, 8, 9, 10, 14, 26, 45, 49, 62, 65, 75, 82, 87
Iconographical 10, 65, 80
Iconography 1, 2, 3, 4, 5, 6, 7, 8, 14, 16, 22, 23, 26, 37, 38, 71, 87
Iconometric 6
Iconometry 7
idol 45, 59, 65, 71, 85
ijyā 15
Image/s 1, 2, 3, 4, 6, 7, 9, 10, 11, 12, 13, 14, 15, 16, 17, 18, 19, 20, 21, 22, 23, 25, 26, 28, 29, 31, 32, 36, 37, 45, 49, 56, 62, 65, 71, 87
image worship 11, 12, 14, 15, 21, 22, 32, 36, 37, 49
immortality 34
imperial 4, 24
incarnation 32, 34, 37

India 2, 3, 6, 8, 9, 10, 11, 14, 16, 17, 21, 22, 23, 28, 29, 32, 33, 34, 36, 37, 38, 39, 65, 75, 86, 87, 88
Indian 2, 3, 6, 7, 9, 10, 14, 17, 19, 23, 32, 33, 38, 87
Indigenous 3, 31
Indo-Arian / s 11
Indra 5
Indus 75
infinite 12
influence 28, 32, 33, 34, 35, 36, 37, 38, 45, 65, 77, 88
Inscription/s 2, 3, 4, 16, 24, 25, 26, 27, 28, 30, 65
insignia 4
installation 6, 7
intact head 42
invasion 33, 34
iron-lance 17
Iron Pillar 24
īśa 12
Islam 34
Islamic 33
īśvara 12
I-tsing 27, 30

J

Jagaddhātri 82
Jaganmātā 45
Jagannātha 32
Jain 38, 49
Jaina 2, 25, 28, 29, 49
Jaina tīrthaṅkara/s 28
Jainavihāra 29
Jainism 28, 65
Jajpur 35
Janārdana 81
Jāṅgulī 38, 53
jaṭāmukuṭa 56
jaws 5
Jāvāladarśanopaniṣat 16
Jayadeva 32, 36
Jayāditya 11
Jewels 49
Jhulelal 75
Jvarāsura 56

K

Kahaum 28
Kalhaṇa 29
Kali era 29
Kālikā 14
kamaṇḍalu 39
Kaṇiṣka 3
Kāntideva 28
Kapardin 5
Kapila 25
Kapileśvara 25
karmakāṇḍa 15
kārmuka 53
Kārtika 30
Kārtikeya 14, 32, 82
kartṛ 42
Kāśikā 11
Kashmir 29
Kāśyapaśilpaśāstra 7
Kātyāyanī 4
Kautsa 25

Kautsaśāva 25, 26
Kāverī 17
Keśava Chatri 35
Keśavasena 30
khaḍga 53
Khoh 25
knees 59
knowledge 2
Kolkata 23
Koṭāla 35
Kriyāsaṃgraha 31
Kṛṣṇa 14, 34
Kṛṣṇakālī 65
Kṛṣñānanda Āgamavāgīśa 8
krura 18, 19
kruramūrti 18
Kubjikāmata 8
kumāra 18, 19
Kumāragupta I 26, 28
kumāramūrti 18
kuṇḍalinī yoga 42
Kūrma 32
Kuṣāṇa 3, 59
Kuśika 25

L

lance 17
lakṣaṇa 20
Lakṣmī 30, 39, 49, 82
Lakulīśaḥ 24
Lalitā 45
leaves 56
liṅga 16, 23, 25
literary 2, 37
literary sources 2, 5
literature 2, 5, 14, 32, 34, 35, 37, 59
Lokeśvara 8, 62
Lord 3, 4, 8, 14, 15, 26, 28, 32, 38, 39, 62, 71, 81, 96
Lotus/es 24, 39, 45, 49, 62, 81
lotus bowl 62
love 24

M

Madanapāla 29
Madhya Predesh 16
Mahābhārata 14, 15, 29, 36, 37, 53
Mahābhāṣya 11, 17
Mahādevī 45
Mahānirvāṇatantra 16
Mahasāmanta 4
Mahāvastu 59
Mahāvīra 4
Mahāyāna 32, 38, 39, 42, 53, 65
Mahāyānī 38, 45, 59, 62
Māheśvara 30
Mahiṣāsuramardinī 26
Makara 75
Mālādhara Basu 37
māna/s 18, 20
Manasā 38, 53
Mānasāra 7
Mānasollāsa 7
maṇḍala 12, 17
Maṇḍana 7, 9
Mandasor Stone Inscription 26
manifest 1, 18, 21

Mankuwar 28
mantra 8, 15
Manu 23
manuscript/s 39, 49
marble 9
materials 2, 5, 7, 15
Mathurā 2, 25, 26, 28
Matsya 6, 8
Maurya 24
Mayamata 7
Mayamuni 7
Mayurbhanj 31
meat 31
medallions 1
mediaeval 9, 35, 37
meditation 15, 17, 27, 33
Meghavarṇa 27
Meharauli Iron Pillar Inscription 24
metal/s 1, 2
milk 35
million Suns 42
miniature 31
M.M. Haraprasad Shastri 31
monarchs 25, 27
monastery/ies 27, 29, 30, 34
monks 27, 30
monotheistic 34
monuments 1, 25
Moon 35
Moon God 13
motherhood 59
Mṛgaśikhāvanam 27
mukti 21
Mukundadāsa 35
mūrti/s 18
Museum/s 3, 10, 23, 32
Muslim/s 33, 34, 35, 36, 38, 75, 77, 81, 82
mystic 36
mysticism 34, 65
mythical 5
mythological 1, 31

N

Nabadwip 71
Nachnakuthara 25
Nadia 71
Nāga 24
Nagod 25
naivedya 15
nara/*s* 11, 18
Nārada 15
Nāradapurāṇa 59
naramūrti 18
Naranārāyaṇa 18
Nārāyaṇa 5, 15, 30, 34, 38
Nārāyaṇapāla 29
Nātha 34
nava tāla 19
neckless 59
nectar 49
Nepal 2
Nepalese 31
Nimbārka 36
nirākāropāsanā 16
Nirguṇa 34
Nirukta 12

Niruktakāra/s 13
Nīti 2
Nītiśāstra 6
non-Arians 56
nondualist 15
non-Purāṇic 56
non-Vedic 56, 62
North 9
Northern 3, 34, 36
North India 9
North-Western 75
nṛpeśas 11
Nṛsiṃha 18
numerous 1, 6, 8, 30
Numismatic/s 2, 3

O

object/s 1, 4, 11, 14, 15, 17, 21
omnibus 6
omnipresent 21, 87
omniscient 62
Orissa 24, 31, 45, 65, 71
ornamentation 2, 6
ornament/s 49, 53, 56, 59, 62, 75

P

Padma 6, 39, 49, 81
Paharpur Copper plate 29
painting/s 1, 2, 7, 10, 14, 16, 49, 59
Pakistan 75
Pāla/s 3, 4, 28, 29
Palm leaf 49
Pāñcālī 80
pañcatāla 19
pañcāyatanapūjā 23
pancopāsanā 23
panentheistic 34
Pāṇini 11, 13, 17
pantheon/s 7, 38, 39, 45, 49, 56, 87
Paramamāheśvara 30, 65
Paramasaugata 4
Paramasaura 30
Paramavaiṣṇava 30, 65
Parameśvara 12, 36, 37
paramount 39
Parāśara 25
parimāṇa 20
parṇapicchikā 56
Parṇaśavarī 38, 56
Pārśvanātha 28
Pārvatī 23, 25
pāśa 53
Pāṭaliputra 26
Patañjali 11, 17, 33
patronage 28, 36, 37
pearls 53
period 2, 3, 5, 9, 16, 25, 26, 28, 32, 37, 59, 77, 88, 100
persecution 65
personification 75
philologist 13
philosopher 36
philosophy 33
pictures 23
pigeon 34
pilgrim/s 28
Pīra-phakira 35

pitcher 56
plastic form 3
Post Christian 32
posture 42, 45
Prabhāvatī 29
Prajñāpāramitā 38, 39
prakṛti 15
pralamba-pāda 59
prasāda 32
pratikṛti 11, 13
pratimā 11
pratimālakṣaṇa 6, 7, 20
Pratimāmāṇalakṣaṇa 7
Pratimānāṭaka 14
pratiṣṭhāvidhi 6
pratyalīḍha 42
preceptor/s 25, 28
Pre Christian 32
premordial nature 59
pre-Vedic 62
primary source 2, 5
principal deity 1
Pṛthivī 13
pūjā 15, 16, 32
Pūjāśīlaprakāra 4
Punjab 34, 36
Purāṇa/s 5, 6, 8, 13, 14, 17, 29
Purānic 2, 5, 6, 13, 31, 39, 59
purification 75
pustaka 39

Q

Queen 29

R

racial 36
Rajasthan 9
Rājataraṅgiṇī 29
Raktāvalī 56
Rāma 18, 34
Rāmāi Paṇḍita 35
Rāmānuja 36
Rāmapūrvatāpanīya 16
Rāmāyaṇa 14, 29
Raṇavaṅkamalla 29
Ratnasambhava 42, 49
raudra 18
Rāvaṇa 19
realization 21, 87
rapprochement 23
reconciliation 23
records 3, 4, 5, 25, 28, 29, 30
reign 25, 27, 28, 35, 36, 37, 65
relief/s 2
religion 24, 25, 28, 32, 33, 37, 59, 65, 88
religious art 1, 2, 6, 8
renunciation 33
respect 5, 6, 7, 9, 14, 29, 30, 31, 34, 37, 45, 65, 86
reverence 29, 86
Ṛgveda 5, 12
Ṛgvedic hymns 5
ritualists 12, 13
rival 23
rivalry 23, 33, 87
rocks 59
rock edict 24

royal 4, 28, 30
Rudra 5, 12, 62
Rudrādhyāya 62
Rudrayāmala 8
Ruler/s 4, 5, 24, 28, 29, 36
rūpa 12
Rūpa Gosvāmī 36
Rūpamaṇḍana 7, 9
rural 38, 53, 56, 59, 77

S

Sadāśiva 4, 30
Sadāśiva mudrā 30
Sādhanamālā 39, 42, 45, 49, 53, 56, 59, 62
*sādhana*s 8, 42, 53
sages 33, 36
Sahajiyā 34
Saint/s 17, 19, 27, 35, 87
Śaiva 6, 17, 23, 24, 25, 29, 30, 32, 34, 65
Śaivism 30, 65
Śākta 6, 23, 25, 29, 38, 65, 71
Śāktatantra 7
Śakti 26, 32, 71
Śaktism 65
Śākyamuni Buddha 3
*Śālagrāma*s 16, 17, 18
samabhaṅga 19
samapāda 19
Samarāṅganasūtradhāra 7
Śambhu 25, 26
Sāṃkhya 33
Samudragupta 4, 27
Sanakānīka 26
Sanātana Gosvāmī 36
Sāncī 1, 24, 25, 28
Sāncī Stone Inscription 24
Śaṅkara 28
Saṅkarṣaṇa 4
śaṅkha 49, 81
Sanskrit 11, 14, 100
Santa 34
śānta 18
Śāntiparvan 15
śara 56
Śāradātilaka 8
Sāranātha 28
Sarasvatī 38, 39
Ṣaṣṭhī 39, 59
*Śāstra*s 10, 21, 22
ṣaṭtāla 18
Satyanārāyaṇa 38, 77, 80, 81
Satyanārāyaṇapūjāvidhi 35
Satyapīra 38, 77, 80, 81
saumya 18
Saura 6, 23, 25, 30
scriptures 39, 42, 53
sculptors 18, 19, 20
sculpture/s 1, 2, 3, 10, 16, 18, 19, 20, 21, 22, 23, 49
sea coast 32
seal/s 1, 2, 4, 30
sect/s 3, 6, 14, 17, 23, 24, 25, 29, 30, 33, 34, 38, 39, 62, 65, 86
sectarian 24, 29, 30, 32, 65, 86, 87
self-denial 33
Sena 3, 4, 28, 30, 65

serpents 53, 62
severed head 42
sheaf of grain 49
shrine/s 1, 4, 27
Siddha/s 27, 34
Śilpa 2
Śilparatna 7
Śilpaśāstra/s 6, 7, 13, 16
Śilpa text/s 7, 49
Siṃhanāda 8, 39, 62
Sindh 75
Sindhi 75
Śitalā 38, 56
Śiva 3, 4, 8, 9, 14, 15, 16, 17, 20, 25, 26, 29, 30, 31, 32, 39, 62
Śivabhāgavata / s 17
Śivaliṅgas 23
śivamātmani paśyanti 16
Śiva-tāṇḍava 20
Skandagupta 28
skulls 42
small pox 56
Smṛti 5, 6, 23
snake-bites 53
snake/s 53, 62
socio-cultural 77
socio-religious 77
ṣoḍaśatāla 18, 19
Someśvaradeva 7
South 9
South Bengal 82
Southern 36
Southern Bengal 5
South India 9, 16
South Indian 9
South-western 31, 34
spiritual 21, 45
spiritualist 33
Śrāvasti 24
Śrī Caitanya Mahāprabhu 36, 37
Śrīgupta 27
Śrīkumāra 7
Śrīlakṣmī 49
Śrīmad Dommanapāla 4, 30
Śrīvidyā 45
Śrīvigraha 15
statuaries 9
Statue/s 2, 59
stone/s 1, 2, 21, 31, 87
stūpa 31
Sufi 33, 34
Sufism 33, 36, 77
Śuklayajurveda 62
Śukranītisāra 6, 20
Sun God 5, 9, 13
Śūnyapurāṇa 35
Suparṇo Garutmān 5
Suprabhedāgama 7
Supreme God 33, 45, 62, 87
Sureśvarī 75
Sūrya 5, 9, 14, 19, 23, 30
Suśipra 5
sūtra 5, 11
svādhyāya 15
swan 39

T

Taittirīyasaṃhitā 12
tāla 18, 19
tambourine 62
Tāmralipta 30
*ṭāṅkā*s 2
Tantra/s 5, 8, 13, 17, 21
Tantrasāra 7, 8
Tāntric 8, 17, 31, 32, 42, 45
tanu 12
Tārā 38, 45
Tārādevī 38
Tārinī 45
tarjanipāśa 56
temple/s 2, 6, 14, 15, 16, 21, 25, 26, 27, 29, 30, 45, 49, 65, 71
terminology 42
terracotta 1, 2
theologies 45
throat 20, 35
throne 59
Tibet 2, 28
Tibetan 30
tiger 82
tiger skin 62
toraṇa 35
tolerance 24, 25, 26, 29, 32, 35, 36, 37, 38, 65
tortoise 31, 45
torque 59
traits 2
transcendental 39
tribhaṅga 19, 20
trident 62
Trideva 62
Tripura 32
Tulasī 17

U

Udayagiri 25, 26
Udayagiri Cave Inscription 24, 25, 28
Uditācārya 25
ugra 18
Umā 19
Universal brotherhood 33
Universe 27
upādāna 15
Upamiteśvara 25
Upamitra 25
Upaniṣadic 12
*Upapurāṇa*s 13
*Upaniṣad*s 34
Ūṣā 5
utpannakrama 42
Uttarakāmikāgama 7

V

vāhana 5
Vaidyadeva 29, 65
Vaikhānasāgama 7
Vainyagupta 29
Vaiṣṇava 6, 17, 23, 25, 26, 29, 30, 34, 36, 37, 65
Vaiṣṇavism 8, 24, 30, 36, 65
Vaiṣṇavite 33, 34, 36, 77
vajra 53
vajraparaśu 56
Vajravarṇanī 42

Vajravairocanī 42
Vajrayāna 3, 8, 9, 31, 42, 49, 65
Vajrayānī 42, 45
Vajrayoginī 38, 42
Vallālasena 31
Vāmana 19
Vanabibi 82
vandalism 33
vapuḥ 12
Varada 49
Varadamudrā 45, 49
Varāhamihira 6, 7
Varman/s 28
Varṇinī 42
Varuṇa 12
Vāsudeva 4, 16
Vāsudeva - Nārāyaṇa - Viṣṇu 5
Vasudhārā 39, 49
Vaṭakṛṣṇa 19
Vāyu 5, 13
Vedas 5
Vedic 2, 5, 11, 12, 14, 15, 62
Vigrahapāla III 29
Vihāra 30
Vijayagupta 37
Vijayasena 65
vilvaphala 49
vimba 11
vīṇā 39, 53
Vināyaka 71
Vināyakī 71
Vīrasena 25, 26
viṣapuṣpa 53
Viśiṣṭādvaitavedānta 36
Viṣṇu 4, 5, 6, 14, 15, 16, 17, 19, 23, 25, 26, 32, 34, 38, 62, 81
Viṣṇudharmottara 8
Viṣṇudharmottarapurāṇa 14, 39
Viśvakarmāvatāraśāstra 7
Viśvarūpasena 30
Viśvavarman 26
Vratakhaṇḍa 6
Vyākhyānamudrā 39
vyakta 18
vyaktāvyakta 17, 18

W

waist 20
wealth 26, 49
West Bengal 71
Western 31, 34, 35
wheat 35
white 5, 39, 53, 56, 62, 81
Wind God 13
wisdom 21, 39
wood-apple 49
woods 1
worship 1, 2, 7, 11, 15, 16, 17, 20, 21, 22, 27, 30, 32, 34, 36, 37, 49, 59, 77, 81, 82
worshipper/s 4, 16, 17, 20, 21, 22, 25

Y

Yājñavalkya 23
yājñika 13
yantra 16, 18
Yāska 12
Yāskācārya 13

Yavana Avatāra 35
yellow 42, 49, 53, 56
yoga 15, 42
Yogadakṣiṇāmūrti 15
Yogāsana 15
Yogasūtra 33
yogī/s 15, 21, 33, 34, 62
yogic 34
yoginī/s 42, 45, 65, 71
Yoginī temple 45, 65, 71

Dr. Sudipa Bandyopadhyay is attached with the Department of Sanskrit, Vidyasagar College, Kolkata as an Associate Professor. She is also offering her lectures to the Department of Sanskrit, University of Calcutta as a Guest Faculty since 2007. She is the Supervisor of M.Phil. & Ph.D. programme of the University of Calcutta since 2009. She is expertise on the area of History, Epigraphy & Palaeography of ancient India. The thrust area of her research project is Science and Technology i.e. Metallurgy, Surgery & Medical treatment, Numismatics, Iconography, Painting and Sculpture, Art and Architecture, Social science as revealed in the glorious civilization of ancient India.

Some of her publications - *'Dharma and War Policy of Ancient India', 'War: Elements of Science in Ancient India', 'Influence of Sentiments (Rasa) in Ancient Indian Painting', 'Iconography and Religious Tolerance', 'Surgery in Ancient India as Revealed in Suśrutasaṃhitā'* and so on. Her only mission is to open the various aspects of the noble and glorious civilization of ancient India.

She wrote an article named *'Surgery in Ancient India and Suśrutasaṃhitā'* which is also a part of the book named 'The History and Philosophy of Science' (eBook ISBN 9781003033448), recently published by 'Routledge India' from London. She has done a UGC – Minor Research Project on *'Iconography and Communal Harmony'*.

Dr. Bandyopadhyay was awarded the 'Shiksharatna' award by the Govt. of West Bengal in 2016.